WHAT CATHOLICS REALLY BELIEVE—
SETTING THE RECORD STRAIGHT

What Catholics Really Believe—Setting the Record Straight

52 Answers to Common Misconceptions about the Catholic Faith

by

Karl Keating

IGNATIUS PRESS   SAN FRANCISCO

Originally published by
Servant Publications
Ann Arbor, Michigan

Cover by Riz Boncan Marsella

Reprinted in 1995
Ignatius Press, San Francisco
ISBN 0–89870–553–3
Library of Congress catalogue number 95-75663
Printed in the United States of America

Contents

Introduction

 Quiz time.
Which of these ten statements are true?

1. Vatican II changed the Church from a monarchy to a democracy.
2. You'll definitely go to heaven if you attend Mass and confess your sins.
3. We now know the Bible contains mistakes.
4. When you get divorced, you're excommunicated and can't receive Communion,
5. Your conscience tells you what's right or wrong.
6. Every Catholic must go to confession at least once a year.
7. An annulment is a divorce for Catholics.
8. You sin if you don't believe in Church-approved apparitions of Mary.
9. Purgatory is no longer a required doctrine.
10. Good works help us earn salvation.

Have you written down your answers? Good—now tear your answer sheet into little bits and throw them away. No matter which of these statements you identified as true, you're wrong. The list doesn't contain even one true statement. All ten are false.

Please forgive the deception. It isn't my intention to embarrass you. (I hope you took this quiz in private, not in front of an audience.) I just want to bring home that even good Catholics can have a less-than-perfect knowledge of their faith.

This little book contains fifty-two misconceptions many Catholics hold—one misconception for each week of the year. The topics, prompted by thousands of questions I've fielded from Catholic audiences over the last four years, range from extraterrestrials to relics, from astrology to reincarnation, from transubstantiation to ecumenism. I discuss the Church and its government, the Bible and its reliability, sacramental practices, Marian doctrines, the hereafter, evangelization, Catholic customs and devotions, and the spirit world.

These fifty-two topics are representative of Catholic confusions, but the list is hardly exhaustive. I was disinclined to write a multi-volume encyclopedia of mistakes, misconceptions, and misunderstandings. My goal in these few pages is simply to entice you to learn more about your faith. After reading this book, you might begin with the books listed in the bibliography. The better you know your Catholic faith, the better you will live it, and the better you live it, the better you will serve Jesus Christ, who is "the way and the truth and the life" (Jn 14:6).

ONE

The Teaching Church and Its Authority

The Teaching Church
and Its Authority

1 | The pope can change doctrine.

Don't tell him that, or you'll get a lecture. He'll explain to you that popes are only guardians of doctrine. They have no power and no desire to change doctrine. Their task is to pass on, in its integrity, the whole corpus of Catholic teaching, and the Holy Spirit protects them in this.

What a pope *can* do, and what many popes have done, is change Church *customs*. Many of these changes have occurred within our own time. Older Catholics recall, for instance, when abstinence from meat was required on Fridays and when Mass was celebrated in Latin rather than in the vernacular. These were not doctrines, but customs. Therefore, they were changeable. As a rough rule of thumb, doctrine concerns *what* we believe, while customs concern *how* we do things. No pope will ever teach that the resurrection was only symbolic, that Jesus' bones are still in the tomb. That would be a change of doctrine, and the Holy Spirit wouldn't stand for it. One hopes Catholics wouldn't either. But a pope theoretically might instruct priests to celebrate Mass no longer in vestments but in top hats and tails. We may hope the Holy Spirit would preserve us from such a foolish decision and visual disaster, but there's no guarantee.

Let me give a further example: We believe Jesus is really present—body, blood, soul, and divinity—in the Eucharist, but Mass may be celebrated in any approved language and in any approved form. If the language of the Mass never could change, we wouldn't even have Latin Masses. After all, Jesus didn't speak Latin, so far as we know, but Aramaic, the common language of Palestine. This was the language Jesus no doubt used at the Last Supper. If the language of the Mass were a matter of doctrine rather than custom, the language couldn't be changed.

2 | Infallibility means that everything the pope says is true.

Don't bet on it. If the pope tells you which team will win the next World Series, keep your money in your pocket. He has no more insight into the outcome of sporting events than you or I do. And if he gives you a list of the best novels of all time, thank him profusely, but feel free to develop your own literary Top Forty.

The pope is infallible, but he isn't a know-it-all. His charism of infallibility, which he enjoys as the successor to Peter, is strictly limited. Vatican I (1869-1870) taught and Vatican II (1962-1965) reaffirmed that the pope teaches infallibly when "he proclaims by a definitive act some doctrine of faith or morals." So states Vatican II's *Dogmatic*

Constitution on the Church. Note the limitation: Papal infallibility extends only to matters of faith or morals—not to Church customs, not to sports, not to literature, not to most things of everyday life. And infallibility comes into play only when the pope "proclaims by a definitive act." This means a formal, public statement. An offhand comment over lunch doesn't count.

By the way, infallibility isn't limited to the pope or to papal decrees. The bishops, when united with the pope in an ecumenical council, also teach infallibly on matters of faith or morals. There have been twenty-one ecumenical councils, and most of them have issued doctrinal or moral decrees. Those decrees are infallible. Many councils have issued disciplinary decrees also, but those decrees are not infallible because they do not concern directly matters of faith or morals.

There is a third mode of infallibility. The pope and the bishops don't have to meet in a council to teach without error. The Holy Spirit guarantees they will teach truly whenever they reiterate what the Church always has taught. The Church always has taught the historical reality of the resurrection, for example, and an individual bishop teaches infallibly when he reiterates this teaching.

3   Vatican II teaches that the Church should be like a democracy. That's why we have parish councils.

If the Council taught that, even the sharpest-eyed readers have failed to find the passage. The Church never has been a democracy and never will be one. Its structure is patterned after the structure of heaven, which is an absolute monarchy with God on the throne. He is the ruler, and we are his subjects. He appointed a prime minister, Peter, to rule in his absence, investing him with much of his own authority as king and shepherd (Mt 16:18-19, Jn 21:15-19). He gave Peter chief assistants, the other apostles. This pattern of government continues today through apostolic succession in the pope and the bishops in union with him.

So why do we have parish pastoral councils? Not because the Church has been changed from a monarchy to a democracy. Remember terms like these properly should be reserved for political institutions only. With respect to the Church they're not quite accurate and should be used only in an accommodated sense. No, pastoral councils have several practical purposes: to relieve parish priests of administrative burdens which can be accomplished as well, often better, by parishioners; to give the pastor feedback from the pews; and to develop a pastoral plan for the parish. In all these the council is a consultative, not a legislative, body. It makes recommendations to the pastor, but doesn't usurp his authority or duties. The pastor cannot abdicate his authority, which comes from the bishop, to a parish council, but he may delegate as much of it as necessary. Of course, he can't delegate his purely sacramental functions, for which ordination is required.

 Vatican II was such a watershed that it's now a waste of time to read books written before the Council.

That attitude is contrary to Vatican II itself. Just look at the notes to the Council's documents—they're packed with references to ancient and medieval writings. The Bible is an ancient writing, remember. Will you therefore drop it from your reading list?

If you insist on regarding Vatican II as a dividing point for your reading, you'd do much better to read only pre-Vatican II books than only post-Vatican II books. Yes, you'd miss recent events, but you'd keep on your shelf the very best of the world's books. Of course, no one today should accept willingly such a silly limitation on reading. People in the past didn't think that way. After Trent (1545-1563), Catholics didn't say, "Let's chuck all the pre-Trent books and read only the modern writers, such as Robert Bellarmine." After Lyons I (1224), they didn't say, "Let's get rid of Augustine and read only this upstart theologian, Thomas Aquinas."

Keep in mind George Santayana's line: "Those who cannot remember the past are condemned to repeat it." This applies to theology too. If you read only modern works, you'll commit ancient errors. This is the tragedy of the New Age movement: It's mired in old errors because those involved in it refuse to look beyond yesterday. It has no historical sense. If it did, it would have more theological sense.

5   The Catholic Church sends people to hell by excommunicating them.

It doesn't. Only God can condemn anyone to hell. That isn't within the Church's power, and no Catholic ever claimed it was. The Church's role is to help people to heaven by teaching and sanctifying. Of course, people can ignore the teaching and reject the grace. If they do and end up in hell, they go there by their own choice.

Excommunication is a Church penalty which excludes a notorious sinner or someone grossly disobedient from the communion of the faithful. It doesn't mean the person ceases to be a Christian. Its purpose is to warn the individual that he risks losing his soul unless he repents.

We've seen examples of excommunication in our own time. In 1953 some bishops in China ordained new bishops without the approval of Pope Pius XII. The ordaining bishops and those they ordained were excommunicated under a provision of canon law which stated that episcopal ordinations may be performed only with the pope's approval. These new bishops had been ordained for the Chinese Patriotic Church, a government-controlled offshoot of the Catholic Church. Other Chinese bishops remained loyal to Rome and found themselves imprisoned —the penalty for loyalty to Church authority.

In 1988 Archbishop Marcel Lefebvre ordained new bishops to oversee the religious society he had founded. The ordinations were done against the wishes of Pope John Paul II, and Archbishop Lefebvre, another ordaining bishop, and the three new bishops were excommunicated automatically. In this case and the Chinese case, people were excommunicated not for teaching heresy, but for gross disobedience.

Excommunication is rarely used nowadays. At one time, it's true, it was used too frequently, and the Council of Trent warned bishops to be more careful in its application. The Council said excommunication must be used sparingly. Its purpose is to bring the wayward back to the practice of the faith and to obedience. If excommunication is wielded crudely, it will lose its effectiveness and may do more harm than good.

Now to a corollary. When Paul said that anyone preaching a heretical gospel would be anathema (Gal 1:8), he didn't condemn the person to hell. He labeled that individual a false teacher. When the Church, in an official decree at a council, accompanies its decisions with anathemas, it's merely doing the same thing as Paul. It's saying, "And anyone who teaches otherwise is a false teacher." It is not condemning anyone to hell.

6 Catholics who leave the Church will go to hell.

Some will, some won't. We don't know the proportions, but leaving the Church is always a blunder.

Let's look first at what makes one a member of the Church. Pope Pius XII put it concisely in his encyclical *Mystici Corporis Christi* (*On the Mystical Body of Christ*, 1943): "Only those are to be accounted really members of the Church who have been regenerated in the waters of baptism, profess the one true faith, and have not cut themselves off from the structure of the Body by their own unhappy act or been severed therefrom, for very grave crimes, by the legitimate authority."

So three things identify the full Catholic: (1) valid reception of the sacrament of baptism, (2) profession of the Catholic faith, and (3) participation in the communion of the Church. By manifesting these marks one comes under the triple office of the Church: priestly (baptism), teaching (confession of faith), and pastoral (obedience to Church authority).

When you were baptized, an indelible mark was placed on your soul. You never need to be baptized again because there's no way to undo your baptism. Not even the worst sin, including heresy and apostasy, can remove a valid baptism. Once baptized, always baptized. (Similarly, once confirmed, always confirmed, and once ordained, always ordained—confirmation and orders also leave indelible marks on the soul.)

Jesus taught that baptism is necessary for entering the kingdom of God (Jn 3:5). In the case of an adult, a profession of faith must precede baptism (Mk 16:16), but young children are exempt because they're incapable of making a profession of faith. They can be baptized anyway and their godparents make a profession of faith for them.

Catholic Tradition has held that those dissociating themselves from the Church voluntarily cease to be full members of the Church. Paul says that after a heretic has been admonished once or twice, he is to be avoided (Ti 3:10). Tertullian, who himself fell into heresy in his later years, wrote that "heretics have no share in our doctrines and the withdrawal from the communion testifies that in any case they are outside of it" (*On Baptism*, 15). Augustine called a heretic a limb "which has been cut off from the body" (*Sermon* 267, 4, 4). In short, neither heretics nor schismatics—those who separate themselves over matters of authority rather than doctrine—are considered full members of the Church.

People leave the Church for various reasons. Some never were "in" it except out of habit. Their faith, if not dead, was a candidate for the intensive care unit. One day they simply stopped going to Mass, and that was that. Others want spiritual nourishment but can't seem to find it in their parishes, so they go elsewhere. There is an irony in this, of course, since the greatest spiritual nourishment is the Eucharist, which is available in every parish, but some people don't really understand what—or, better, who—the Eucharist is. They leave the Church for a denomination that seems to be "alive."

Still others leave in good faith, thinking—wrongly, of course—that the Catholic faith is untrue and some other faith is true. If they and the others don't realize their actions are wrong, they remain related to the Church spiritually, even though they cease to be legal members of it. They still may achieve justification and salvation, but these are harder to achieve the further one distances oneself from the complete truth, found only in the Catholic Church, and the ordinary sources of grace, the sacraments. Leaving the Church, even with the best of intentions, is a great blunder because, all things else being equal, the move diminishes one's chances for heaven.

If people leave in bad faith—if they leave knowing full well the Catholic Church is the one founded by Jesus and that they ought to be members of it and believe all its doctrines without exception—then they have adopted for their motto what Dante put above the gates of hell: "Abandon all hope ye who enter here." No one knowingly abandoning the truth and failing to repent can be saved.

 The Church teaches that as long as Catholics go to Mass and confess any serious sin, they will go to heaven.

It isn't enough to believe the Catholic faith—you also have to live it. In fact, *how* you live demonstrates *what* you believe. If you have what is termed "saving faith," it will manifest itself in a holy, obedient life. If your faith is nothing more than a list of propositions to which you give mental assent, you have only intellectual faith, the kind James says is insufficient for salvation (Jas 2:24). Notice that Paul calls real Christian faith "the obedience of faith" (Rom 1:5, 16:26). It's a faith which manifests itself in proper acts.

If you deliberately skip Mass, you are disobedient to legitimate Church authority, which commands weekly attendance, and you renege on your chief obligation as a creature: worship of your Creator. If you don't confess serious (mortal) sins, you are not really sorry for them. After all, if you really are sorry for your sins, you will humble yourself by confessing them in the way God has ordained, though sacramental confession (Jn 20:22-23). If you refuse to confess your serious sins, you have only a pretended sorrow and remain grace-less. Without grace, you can't go to heaven.

Don't look at attending Mass or confessing sins as just two of many different things you need to do to be counted as saved. Salvation isn't a matter of accumulating brownie points. Some Catholics think God weighs their lives in a scale: if their good deeds outweigh their bad deeds, they go to heaven. This is incorrect. Someone might live a totally immoral life, repent just before dying, and then be saved, even though the evil deeds of a lifetime "outweigh" the single good deed of repentance. Someone else might live a nearly sinless life, and then, in the last hour, sin mortally and die unrepentant. A lifetime of good deeds will not make up for final impenitence.

Then why bother to be good? Because we are creatures of habit. If we are in the habit of doing good, we likely will continue to do good and stay out of sin. If we are in the habit of doing evil, we likely will continue to do evil and will die in a sinful, unrepentant state. Sin even affects our intellects. The more we sin, the less clearly we think. If we think badly, we act badly. It's the most vicious of circles. If we live virtuously, we think more clearly because grace helps elevate the mind. Our good thinking leads to good living.

8 | We shouldn't spend money on building fancy churches.

That may be your view, but it hasn't been the view of most Catholics through the centuries. The Church has been around a long time and has been the recipient of the love and gifts of millions of Catholics. Take a look at an older church in your city. It's probably ornate. The rich decorations were donated by members of the parish in praise of and in thanksgiving to God and in honor of the saints. Catholics believe there's much sense in ecclesiastical art, so we've always been generous in underwriting lovely churches—this was especially true of Catholics who lived some generations or centuries ago and who, though poor by today's standards, took pride in making the house of God a real house, not just a barn.

In the Middle Ages peasants contributed, as their means permitted, to the erection and maintenance of their cathedrals. Some labored in stone and brick, others hauled lumber, some prepared meals for the workers. The best architects and stonemasons vied for the honor of constructing magnificent churches. In many towns construction lasted decades, sometimes centuries, and much of the labor was donated.

In this the people followed Scripture. Recall that God ordered the Jews to build a magnificent temple in Jerusalem (2 Sm 7:13). Jesus commended the poor widow for contributing to the upkeep of the temple (Lk 21:2). He rebuked Judas, who complained about using precious oil in Jesus' honor instead of selling it and giving the proceeds to the poor (Jn 12:3-5). All this argues in favor of the churches some people disparage. Remember: Jesus is God and is entitled to our worship, and worship can be enhanced through magnificent surroundings. We're spirit and body, and the body has senses, and it makes sense to make use of those senses in worship. One way to do that is to use finely appointed churches.

I recall visiting the impressive parish church in Mount Angel, Oregon, a small town settled by immigrants in the nineteenth century. They erected what may be the loveliest church on the West Coast. Its intricate wood carvings and stunning ceiling reminded me, as no bare-bones church could, that the greatest beauty found on Earth pales next to God's own beauty. This little-known church, now protected from "renovation" by being designated a state historic site, did precisely what good architecture should do—it raised my mind to God.

While praying there I was reminded how Paul Claudel, French poet, playwright, and diplomat, was brought back to the practice of the faith while visiting Notre Dame Cathedral in Paris. The beauty of the building and of the liturgy brought to his mind the beauty of God. In some inexplicable way a mental stumbling block was removed, and he became again a fervent and pious Catholic.

Keep in mind that the construction of fine churches never seems to undermine contributions to the poor. In fact, the more generous people are toward God—and one way of being generous toward him is by praising him through great architecture—the more generous they are toward other people. Perhaps you have noticed that it's almost exclusively the rich who complain about fancy churches, while it's the un-rich who contribute to their building and upkeep, just as it is the un-rich who give the bulk of the funds which keep charitable causes afloat. The poor boxes in Catholic churches are filled mainly by the offerings of the poor.

TWO

The Bible —Its Inerrancy and Authenticity

The Bible—Its Inerrancy and Authenticity

9	**B**efore modern times, lay people weren't allowed to read the Bible.

Let's face it. When we hear the term "Bible Christian," we don't usually think of Catholics. Yet no one has a better right to the term, since the Bible is a Catholic book written *for* Catholics, and it is interpreted infallibly only by the teaching authority vested by Jesus in the Catholic Church.

So why do we tend to think of the Bible as "Protestant"? Probably because the Protestant Reformers of the sixteenth century claimed the Bible as their sole rule of faith. They rejected the teaching authority of the Church. No longer was faith to be determined by Scripture *plus* Tradition, but by Scripture alone—even though this itself was an unscriptural principle. Human nature being what it is, out of reaction to Protestantism's claims many Catholics deemphasized the Bible, leaving it to "experts" and Church officials, while Protestants, who abandoned the Mass, turned to the Bible for daily spiritual sustenance.

Some people think this anomalous position was encouraged by the Church. This is a common misconception, one even Catholics hold. It is easily disproved. We can go back to Pope Pius XII's 1943 encyclical on promoting biblical studies. This document may be found at the beginning of many Catholic Bibles, and it fairly begs Catholics to immerse themselves in Scripture. We can go back to Pope Leo XIII's 1893 encyclical on the study of Scripture. It demonstrates that a complete Catholic is a biblical Catholic. We can go that far back, but that's only a century. We can go much further. From the earliest times popes and councils, saints and scholars, have encouraged Bible reading. It is unfortunate that the upheavals of the sixteenth century have obscured this point.

One charge leveled against the Church for years has been that the Church chained the Bible, ostensibly to keep it away from the people. Both Catholics and Protestants are surprised to learn that the Church indeed chained the Bible—but for exactly the opposite reason. In the Middle Ages and into the early years of the printing press, Bibles were scarce and expensive. Each was copied by hand, and many sported illuminated pages. A single Bible could be worth ten thousand dollars in today's currency. Often a town had a single book, and that book was the Bible.

Kept in the parish church, that Bible was made available to lay Catholics by chaining it to the table on which it was placed, just as telephone books today are kept available for the public by chaining them to telephone booths. Does the phone company chain the Yellow Pages so no one can use them? Quite the opposite—so the maximum number of people can have access to them. It was the same with the Bible. In fact, after the English Reformation, the Bible was chained in churches which had not previously displayed copies. So, if Catholic authorities are to be blamed for chaining the Bible, Protestant authorities should be blamed as well. In fact, both should be praised, not blamed.

Many people are under the impression that Luther was the first to make the Bible available in the vernacular and that the Bible had been kept in Latin so lay folks couldn't make use of it. Doubly wrong. *The New Catholic Encyclopedia* notes, "There was no want of early German translations of Scripture." If we count just printed versions (Johann Gutenberg, a Catholic, produced the first printed Bible—with Church approval—in 1455; Luther was born in 1483), eighteen German editions of the whole Bible appeared prior to the posting of Luther's Ninety-Five Theses (1517), which signaled his break with Rome. The first of these was printed in 1466. The first printed Flemish edition appeared in 1477. Two Italian versions were printed in 1471. A Catalan Spanish edition came out in 1478. The first printed edition in Polish was made in 1516, a year before Luther posted his theses. The earliest English edition was printed in 1525.

Keep in mind these are all printed editions of the *entire* Bible. Printed editions of certain books of the Bible appeared somewhat earlier, and manuscript editions of the whole Bible or of individual books appeared in vernacular languages centuries earlier.

The earliest precursor to the English-language Bible was a paraphrase of Genesis written around 670 in Anglo-Saxon by Caedmon. Bede, who died in 735, translated into Anglo-Saxon at least the Gospel of John. There were several editions of the Bible in Middle English, the language of Geoffrey Chaucer's *Canterbury Tales.* The best book on this subject, now out of print but worth a trip to the library, is Fr. Hugh Pope's *English Versions of the Bible.*

Just as it is wrong to think Luther was the first to put the Bible into the vernacular—he was a good millennium too late—so it is wrong to think the Bible was kept in Latin so common people couldn't read it. Until sometime in the nineteenth century, every well-schooled person in the West could read Latin, and at the time of the Reformation nearly everyone who could read at all could read Latin, which for years after Luther was still a "live" language, not just in the Church but also in diplomacy and in literature. Samuel Johnson, who died in 1784, wrote many fine poems in Latin and wasn't considered old fashioned for doing so. Since nearly all readers read Latin, keeping the Bible in Latin was no burden and certainly did nothing to stifle the circulation of Scripture.

10 Because of ecumenism, Catholics may now read any Bible translation.

Yes and no. No one will rap you on the wrist if you pick up a Protestant translation, but, unless you're well-versed in biblical studies, you'll do yourself a disservice if you rely on any translation not approved by the Church.

First of all, you'll probably be missing the seven deuterocanonical books, which means the Old Testament you'll be reading will have only thirty-nine books, not the full forty-six.

Second, you'll be reading accompanying notes not

necessarily in harmony with Catholic teaching. If you know our teaching well, you can profit by seeing what Protestants believers think, but if your understanding of the Catholic faith isn't rock-solid, you might find yourself picking up, perhaps unconsciously, notions which aren't compatible with Catholic doctrines.

If you're going to read only one Bible, make sure it's a Catholic translation with Catholic notes. Even that doesn't mean you won't have to keep your eyes open, of course. There is no ideal translation, and no Catholic Bible now on the market has notes which can't be criticized by someone—after all, translators and note-writers, being human, sometimes express themselves poorly.

11   Only priests or qualified religious can teach Scripture classes.

Says who? The popes have never imposed such a limitation, nor has any Vatican department. Such a limitation would be imposed only if priests and religious—and no one else—had a duty to spread the faith, but that isn't the case. We are all called to accept truth, to live it, and to spread it. The Great Commission (Mt 28:19-20) was given in a special way to the apostles, but it applies to all of us.

One of the ways we can engage in evangelization is through teaching our fellow parishioners about the Bible. (Augustine said that people who are ignorant of the Gospels are ignorant of Christ—good to keep in mind.) In each parish, if only we look for them, are lay people who are well-versed—no pun intended—in Scripture and able to convey accurately the Church's understanding of Scripture to the class.

Sometimes priests and religious are the best instructors, sometimes not. I received a letter from a woman at whose parish a nun was teaching an introductory course in Catholic beliefs and in Scripture. When some students said they wanted her to be more specific about which doctrines were true and which weren't, she insisted that truth is relative and that searching for truth is a waste of time.

She capped her argument by saying, "As Jesus asked, 'What is truth?'" The students' jaws dropped. They were not impressed that their instructor—supposedly familiar with Scripture—put into Jesus' mouth the words of Pontius Pilate (Jn 18:38). Jesus had earlier given a ready answer to Pilate's question: "I am the way and the truth and the life" (Jn 14:6).

12 The Gospels contain lots of inconsistencies.

What do you mean by "inconsistencies"? Outright contradictions? There aren't any. Passages that seem to be saying different things? There are some, but they can be harmonized—that is, they can be read together to make a sensible account.

Consider the incident in which Jesus heals two blind men outside Jericho. In Matthew 20:29-34 the men are unnamed and are healed as Jesus leaves the city. In Mark 10:46-52 only one blind man, Bartimaeus, is mentioned, and he is healed as Jesus leaves the city. In Luke 18:35-43 only one blind man is mentioned, but he is not named, and he seems to be healed as Jesus enters the city, not as he leaves it.

Certainly all these passages refer to the same incident, so how can the two apparent inconsistencies (one man versus two, entering the city versus leaving it) be reconciled? Here is one way: Bartimaeus called out to Jesus as he and the crowd entered Jericho, but in the commotion Bartimaeus was not heard. By the time Jesus left the city, Bartimaeus had been joined by another blind man. Only Bartimaeus' name is recorded, perhaps because of his persistence, perhaps because he later became well known in the Christian community. Bartimaeus calls out again and this time is heard because the crowd is now subdued. Jesus cures him and the other man.

Here is another apparent inconsistency. In Matthew 20:20-21 the mother of James and John approached Jesus and asked that her sons might sit at his right and left when he came into his kingdom. In Mark 10:35-37 James and John themselves made the request. Which evangelist are we to believe? Both. There is no inconsistency. The mother of James and John first approached Jesus, paving the way for her sons to come later and second the request. We see something similar in 1 Kings 1:11-21. Nathan first had Solomon's mother, Bathsheba, approach the aged King David with the news that Adonijah was seizing power. Then Nathan himself went to the King with the same information.

Now consider you're taking a vacation. You go to Hawaii and on the way home stop at the Grand Canyon. You tell one friend, "On my vacation I went to Hawaii." You tell another, "On my vacation I visited the Grand Canyon." If the friends compare notes, they'll find an apparent inconsistency. Surely they'll conclude, "Well, he must have gone to both places. After all, going to one doesn't exclude going to the other." So it is with the Gospel stories.

We find what appear to be inconsistencies, but they appear such only because the Gospels are themselves fragmentary accounts of Christ's life, each account including different fragments.

13 All right, but the Old Testament has lots of contradictions and people have known that for at least a century.

The very first thing you need to understand about the Bible is that it is not just one single book. It is a collection of books, composed by dozens of people living hundreds of years apart under quite varying circumstances. Although God is the principal author of the Bible, the human authors worked freely. God did not reduce them to automatons or even to secretaries taking dictation. They brought to their writing all their insight and their lack of insight, all their literary skills and their absence of literary skills. God respected their natural abilities, while he used them for a supernatural purpose.

Some of the Old Testament writers wrote straight history, as is found in the books of Kings and Maccabees. Others wrote poetry, as in the psalms or in that long love poem, The Song of Songs. Still others drafted what might loosely be called biographical sketches, such as the books of Ruth and Judith. There were other literary forms as well.

The one thing no one wrote, in either the Old or the New Testament, was a theological treatise or a catechism. Although the Bible is inspired and contains revealed teaching, that teaching is not set out systematically. God has expressed truth in a multiplicity of ways. Sometimes this multiplicity can be misconstrued by unfriendly readers. Consider a well-known instance.

William Henry Burr's *Self-Contradictions of the Bible* was published in 1859, and it was reprinted as recently as 1987. Some people, especially those styling themselves "rationalists," still find its arguments convincing. Even Catholics are bamboozled into thinking Burr and his descendants are on to something, but only someone ignorant of the Bible could think pairings such as these are telling blows against Scripture:

"There died of the plague twenty-four thousand: 'And those that died in the plague were twenty and four thousand'" (Num 25:9). "There died of the plague but twenty-three thousand: 'And fell in one day three and twenty thousand'" (1 Cor 10:8). These verses are in perfect harmony because they are both approximations. When police estimate a crowd at fifteen thousand, they may well mean anywhere from ten thousand to twenty thousand—the order of magnitude is correct, and that's all that's needed. Another effort by Burr: "A good name is a blessing: 'A good name is better than precious ointment'" (Eccl 7:1)."A good name is a curse: 'Woe unto you when all men shall speak well of you'" (Lk 6:26). Again, no contradiction. The second verse refers not so much to a good name, but to praise by the public. One can have a bad reputation—or, more precisely, one's acts may result in a bad reputation—yet be praised by people whose reputations, if they have any at all, are no better. Evil people praise evil people—praise doesn't turn the objects of the praise into good people.

The Bible appears to be full of contradictions only if

you approach it in the wrong way. If you think it is supposed to be a listing of theological propositions, you won't make heads or tails of it. If you think it is written in the literary forms you're most familiar with, you'll go astray in interpreting it. Your only safe bet is to read it with the mind of the Church, which affirms the Bible's inerrancy. If you do that, you'll see that it contains no fundamental contradictions because, being God's inspired Word, it's wholly true and can't be anything else.

14 Catholics don't believe in the inerrancy of the Bible. That is what Protestants believe, especially Fundamentalists.

I can't speak for every Catholic, but I can tell you what the Catholic Church teaches. As you know, there are Catholics who have not conformed themselves to the mind of the Church. The *Dogmatic Constitution on Divine Revelation,* issued by the bishops at Vatican II, says, "[S]ince everything asserted by the inspired authors or sacred writers must be held to be asserted by the Holy Spirit, it follows that the books of Scripture must be acknowledged as teaching firmly, faithfully, and *without error* that truth which God wanted put into the sacred writings for the sake of our salvation" (emphasis mine).

This means, for instance, that when the Bible ascribes a miracle to Jesus, he really performed that miracle. We are not to conclude that overzealous Christians of later years inserted the account into the text because the story seemed pleasing to pious ears. In short, the Bible is trustworthy. Of course, passages must be read in context, and for a proper understanding we must perceive the literary forms. We must take poetry as poetry, not history, and history as history, not poetry.

The Council Fathers reminded us that, "For the correct understanding of what the sacred author wanted to assert, due attention must be paid to the customary and characteristic styles of perceiving, speaking, and narrating which prevailed at the time of the sacred writer."

Common sense can take us a long way. When a sacred writer says "the sun rose," we don't have to conclude the Bible is teaching us that the earth is the center of the solar system and the sun orbits the earth. When Genesis tells us that everything was created in six days, we don't have to conclude these were six days of twenty-four hours, since Genesis is using a certain literary form, akin to poetry, to convey the truth that God created everything out of nothing and gave order to his creation. Many Fundamentalists go overboard on literalness because they have no recourse to an infallible interpreter (that is, the Catholic Church) and must fall back on their own interpretive powers, and many self-styled moderns go overboard by claiming we have to "demythologize" the Bible. We should avoid both extremes. We don't need to collapse into either a crass literalism which makes no use of literary forms or into an anti-miraculism which tosses out everything smacking of the supernatural.

15	**M**odern Scripture scholarship has shown the New Testament was written well after the events took place. The miracle stories

are—like fisherman's tales—probably exaggerated and legendary.

Sit down, please, while you're introduced to some of the latest scholarship. Yes, you're correct that many scholars, both Catholic and Protestant, say the books of the New Testament were written so late, perhaps even into the second century, that they couldn't have been written by the men whose names they bear. The scholars' conclusions are often tendentious; they are opinions drawn, all too often, from a bias against miracles. If something supernatural appears in Scripture, their prejudice is to assume it must have been a late interpolation, not an accurate account of what really happened.

This position relies largely on the theory that the Gospels were written many years after the events they described—so long after, in fact, that errors and legends crept into the reporting. But in the last few years top-flight scholars have unearthed information which suggests a new understanding, that the New Testament books, particularly the Gospels, were composed very early.

French scholar Claude Tresmontant, for instance, posits that Matthew's Gospel may have been written in Hebrew, later translated into Greek, within a few years of the resurrection. The late Jean Carmignac came up with early dates also, as did the late liberal Anglican scholar, Bishop John A.T. Robinson, who concluded, in his 1976 book *Redating the New Testament*, that all the books of the New Testament were written prior to the destruction of Jerusalem, which occurred in A.D. 70.

The dating of New Testament books has been a roller coaster ride. A century or two ago scholars thought many of the books had been written in the second century, contradicting the ancient view that each book was written by an apostle or the disciple of an apostle within a few decades of the resurrection. As Scripture scholarship advanced—by fits and starts, but mainly by fits—datings were thrust backward, closer to the ancient position. If Tresmontant, Carmignac, and Robinson are right in their views, even some of the ancient writers will appear to be "late daters," and the miraculous stories will be seen as coming from eyewitnesses or from those who obtained their information from eyewitnesses.

Redating the New Testament was politely but not, for the most part, enthusiastically reviewed in the scholarly journals. What could one expect? People who had staked their reputations on dating the New Testament as late as possible—even, parts of it, well into the second century—were displeased that someone not able to be classified as a reactionary should come up with answers Augustine would have been comfortable with.

Robinson "worked from an exclusively historical methodology," wrote Jean Carmignac in *The Birth of the Synoptics*. "I work with a methodology which is principally philological but historical on occasion"—that is, Carmignac based his studies mainly on the meaning and history of words. A Dead Sea Scrolls translator and an expert in the Hebrew in use at the time of Christ, he reached conclusions similar to Robinson's, but he came at the problem from a different angle. He translated the synoptic Gospels "backwards," from Greek into Hebrew. He was astonished at what he found.

"I wanted to begin with the Gospel of Mark. In order to facilitate the comparison between our Greek Gospels and the Hebrew text of Qumran, I tried, for my own personal use, to see what Mark would yield when translated back into the Hebrew of Qumran. I had imagined that this translation would be difficult because of considerable differences between Semitic thought and Greek thought, but I was absolutely dumbfounded to discover that this translation was, on the contrary, extremely easy. Around the middle of April 1963, after only one day of work, I was convinced that the Greek text of Mark could not have been redacted directly in Greek, and that it was in reality only the Greek translation of an original Hebrew."

Carmignac had planned for enormous difficulties, but they didn't arise. He discovered the Greek translator of Mark had slavishly kept to the Hebrew word order and grammar. Could this have been the result of a Semite writing in Greek, a language he didn't know too well and on which he imposed Hebrew structures? Or could the awkward phrasings found in our Greek text have been nothing more than overly faithful translations, perhaps "transliterations" would be more accurate, of Semitic originals? If the second possibility were true, then we have synoptic Gospels written by eyewitnesses at a very early date.

Carmignac spent most of the next twenty-five years meticulously translating the Greek into Hebrew and making endless comparisons. *The Birth of the Synoptics* is a popular summary of what he hoped to publish in a massive multi-volume set. It is a delightful shocker of a book. Consider just one example. (Carmignac gives many, but his short book isn't weighed down with them.) The Benedictus, the song of Zachary, is given in Luke 1:68-79. In Greek, as in English, the Benedictus, as poetry, seems unexceptional. There is no evidence of clever composition. But when it is translated into Hebrew, a little marvel appears.

In the phrase "to show mercy to our fathers," the expression "to show mercy" is the Hebrew verb *hanan*, which is the root of the name *Yohanan* (John). In "he remembers his holy covenant," "he remembers" is the verb *zakar*, which is the root of the name *Zakaryah* (Zachary). In "the oath which he swore to our father Abraham" is found, for "to take an oath," the verb *shaba*, which is the root of the name *Elishaba* (Elizabeth).

"Is it by chance," asks Carmignac, "that the second strophe of this poem begins by a triple allusion to the names of the three protagonists: John, Zachary, Elizabeth? But this allusion only exists in Hebrew; the Greek or English translation does not preserve it."

Carmignac gives many other examples, and he draws these conclusions about the dating of the synoptics: "The latest dates that can be admitted are around A.D. 50 for Mark... around 55 for Completed Mark, around 55-60 for Matthew, between 58 and 60 for Luke. But the earliest dates are clearly more probable: Mark around 42, Completed Mark around 45, (Hebrew) Matthew around 50, (Greek) Luke a little after 50." These dates are all approximate, of course, particularly those for Mark and Matthew, and they are the result of Carmignac's mainly philological analysis.

Claude Tresmontant, in *The Hebrew Christ*, working parallel to Carmignac but with a different methodology, comes up with these datings: Matthew, early 30s, within a few years of the resurrection; Luke 40-60; Mark 50-60. Carmignac keeps to the view that Mark was composed first, while Tresmontant thinks Matthew preceded Mark.

Regardless, each denies what is the majority opinion among biblical scholars, that the synoptics were written late in the first century, possibly into the last decade or two.

Carmignac draws a few other conclusions. He says that the Gospels of Mark and Matthew and the documents on which Luke based his Gospel were written in a Semitic language, either Aramaic or Hebrew, but he says Hebrew is the more likely. What is more, the Gospel of Mark probably was written first in Hebrew by Peter, with Mark acting as Peter's secretary. Then this Gospel was translated into Greek, possibly with changes by Mark, around the year 63. This Gospel has preserved the name of the translator rather than that of the original author.

As he wrote *The Birth of the Synoptics*, Carmignac suspected his "scientific arguments [would] prove reassuring to Christians and [would] attract the attention and interest of non-believers. But they overturn theories presently in vogue and therefore they will be fiercely criticized." Truly honest scholars will have to grapple with what Carmignac has come up with. Others will continue where he left off. It may be, a few decades from now, that the "assured results of modern biblical scholarship" will look different from what we have been told to accept as gospel truth.

THREE

✠ The Mass
and ✠
the Sacraments

The Mass and
the Sacraments

<table>
<tr><td>**16**</td><td>**Anyone who wants to can receive Communion at Mass.**</td></tr>
</table>

Incorrect. In 1986 the National Conference of Catholic Bishops issued guidelines for receiving Communion. These guidelines are printed on the back cover of many missalettes. The bishops said, "Catholics fully participate in the celebration of the Eucharist when they receive Holy Communion in fulfillment of Christ's command to eat his body and drink his blood. In order to be disposed properly to receive Communion, communicants should not be conscious of grave sin, have fasted for an hour, and seek to live in charity and love with their neighbors. Persons conscious of grave sin must first be reconciled with God and the Church through the sacrament of penance. A frequent reception of the sacrament of penance is encouraged for all."

Two things here especially need to be noted. First, you must be in a state of grace to receive Communion. If you aren't, you commit sacrilege, which is irreverence toward what is sacred. Sacrilege is a sin (1 Cor 11:27). Unworthy reception of Communion, therefore, not only doesn't give you any graces, but it give you a bigger spiritual deficit— better to remain quietly in the pew.

What is grave sin? A grave sin is the same thing as a serious sin or a mortal sin. We call such a sin mortal because it mortally wounds the soul by driving out sanctifying grace. A person guilty of a mortal sin is disqualified from heaven and is said to lose justification. Mortal sins include any serious infractions of the "Seven Deadlies" (pride, covetousness, lust, anger, gluttony, envy, sloth). The most popular sins in our culture are among those which disqualify one from receiving Communion: abortion, contraception, adultery, fornication. A mortal sin is any sin which fulfills three conditions: (1) It involves a serious matter, (2) you give your full consent to it, and (3) you have time for sufficient reflection on its seriousness—even a few seconds may be enough. If any of these conditions is absent, your act is either a venial sin or no sin at all.

Note the bishops' emphasis on frequent confession. All recent popes have gone to confession weekly. Safe to say, they have lived better than most of us, which suggests we need to confess more often than most of us are accustomed to. Confessing only once a year—or even less often—would seem to be the right frequency only for those nearly incapable of sin. In fact, some people seem convinced they have been immaculately conceived and therefore don't sin—they only make mistakes! Or they are so inert they can't work up the energy to do anything, sinful or otherwise.

If popes realize the need to confess weekly, perhaps the

rest of us should confess at least monthly, which happens to be the frequency most spiritual directors or advisors recommend. People who have not been to confession in more than a year probably should think long and hard about whether they qualify for Communion. We shouldn't receive Communion just because everyone else seems to. Communion is not a social event, but an intimate union with God. If we have been away from confession a long time, we should start to wonder whether our sensitivity to sin has been blunted. If we do not feel sinful, it may be that our spiritual senses have been clouded by sin. In other words, the less sinful we feel, the more we may need confession.

So much for Catholics. Here are the bishops' guidelines for other Christians who attend Mass: "We welcome to this celebration of the Eucharist those Christians who are not fully united with us. It is a consequence of the sad divisions in Christianity that we cannot extend to them a general invitation to receive Communion. Catholics believe that the Eucharist is an action of the celebrating community signifying a oneness in faith, life, and worship of the community. Reception of the Eucharist by Christians not fully united with us would imply a oneness which does not yet exist and for which we must all pray."

Note that the bishops say "we cannot extend to [other Christians] a general invitation to receive Communion." But some Christians of other traditions may be given Communion by a Catholic priest under special circumstances. The regulations are found in the Code of Canon Law. Canon 844, section 3, says, "Catholic ministers may licitly administer the sacraments of penance, Eucharist, and anointing of the sick to members of the oriental churches which do not have full communion with the Catholic Church, if they ask on their own for the sacraments and are properly disposed. This holds also for members of other churches, which in the judgment of the Apostolic See are in the same condition as the oriental churches as far as these sacraments are concerned."

The "oriental churches" are the Eastern Orthodox churches, which have authentic bishops and priests and which have all seven sacraments. These churches are in schism from the Catholic Church, dating back to 1054. Their doctrines are almost identical to ours. The Catholic Church allows Eastern Orthodox to receive Communion at a Catholic Mass if they ask for it.

What about the "other churches" which "are in the same condition as the oriental churches"? These would be churches which believe as Catholics do regarding the Eucharist and the other sacraments—and that eliminates all Protestant churches which are likely to come to mind. As a practical matter, then, Protestants may not receive Communion at Mass.

A postscript: The bishops also mention welcoming non-Christians to Mass, noting that they can't receive Communion, but asking them to unite themselves with us in prayer.

 17 **V**atican II emphasized the spirit instead of the letter of the law, so we are not obliged to attend Sunday Mass anymore.

This assumes there is a conflict between the spirit and the letter. Vatican II nowhere suggests this, and it remains one of the six precepts of the Church that Catholics must attend Mass on Sundays and holy days, unless a proportionate reason, such as illness, prevents their attendance.

Why has the Church made such a rule? Because we're creatures, and the very first duty of a creature—at least of a creature possessing intelligence and will—is to worship its Creator. But we are creatures with *free* will, and this poses a problem. Free will can be freely abused—and often is. All of our sins arise from an abuse of free will. Our fallen nature being what it is, many of us would skip Mass if attendance were not required. In insisting that we attend, the Church is doing us a great favor. It is saving us from our own laziness. It would prefer that we go of our own accord, without any sort of coercion, but the Church is realistic. It knows human nature.

Look at what Paul said about the spirit and the letter: "But now we are released from the law, dead to what held us captive, so that we may serve in the newness of the spirit and not under the obsolete letter" (Rom 7:6). If read out of context and with the modern understanding of "spirit versus letter," this seems like permission to do anything. It is not that at all. If the letter is demanding and restrictive, the spirit is even more so. What Paul means is that the good Christian will *want* to do what he is supposed to do, and he will do it out of love of God, not out of fear of punishment.

Consider the analogy of the forgiveness of sins in confession. You will have your sins forgiven if you manifest at least imperfect contrition, which is sorrow for your sins arising out of fear of God's punishment. That is a sufficient motive, but it is not the ideal. You should strive for perfect contrition, which is sorrow arising out of your having offended God. Obedience to the letter of the law might be likened to imperfect contrition. It is good enough that you follow God's law merely because you want to avoid trouble, but that is not the ideal. It is better to do what you should do—that is, to follow the spirit of the law or the purpose behind the law—without always looking over your shoulder for a spiritual constable.

18 | Jesus dies and is sacrificed again at every Mass.

In the old days—say, more than twenty years ago—the only people who claimed this were Fundamentalists. Today even some Catholics think that at each Mass Jesus dies just as he died once on Calvary and that his sacrifice is replayed from scratch. We probably can attribute Catholics thinking this not so much to the industrious work of Fundamentalist proselytizers, but to Catholics' own poor catechetical formation. The sad fact is that most Catholics, of all ages, are so poorly catechized that they can't explain to other Christians very much about their own faith. This shows especially in their discussion of the Mass. Their thinking is so hazy that they unknowingly concur with Fundamentalist opponents of the Church.

Here are the facts in brief: Jesus does not die again at each Mass. As Scripture explains, he died only once (Heb 7:27, 9:12, 9:25-28, 10:10-14). His one-time death was sufficient to atone for all our sins. He gave himself up voluntarily to be killed—he was a willing sacrifice. "Christ loved us and handed himself over for us as a sacrificial offering to God" (Eph 5:2). He "offered one sacrifice for sins" (Heb 10:12).

In the Mass the sacrifice of Calvary is re-presented, not

in a bloody, physical way, but in an unbloody, sacramental way. Christ's blood was shed only once, but it is continually offered to the Father. When a priest offers the sacrifice of the Mass, he is not offering a sacrifice distinct from that on Calvary. Christ is not dying all over again. What is on the altar is the very same sacrifice as on Calvary, but it is made present to us today in a special, sacramental way. This is a presence distinct from a physical, historical presence and distinct from a merely symbolic presence. It is a third kind of presence. In it Christ is really present on the altar, and at the consecration a real offering of Christ to the Father is made. Although Christ died only once, through the Mass his saving act is made actually present, day by day, until the end of the world.

19 Lutherans and Anglicans believe in the Real Presence in the same way we Catholics do. They just explain it differently.

Wrong. Consubstantiation is the belief, held by some Protestants, particularly Lutherans and Anglicans, that in the Eucharist, after the consecration, the substances of both the body and blood of Christ and of bread and wine remain. The body and blood are "with the substance" (*con-substantia*) of the bread and wine, sitting right next to them, so to speak. Transubstantiation is quite different. It is the belief that the whole substance of bread and wine is converted or literally changed into the whole substance of the body and blood of Christ, with only the appearance (the accidents, as theologians say) or sensible qualities of the former remaining. Consubstantiation means the Eucharist consists of the body and blood of

Christ, *plus* the bread and wine. Transubstantiation means only the body and blood are present, although the appearances of bread and wine remain as sacramental symbols of earthly food.

The term transubstantiation was decided upon at the Fourth Ecumenical Council of the Lateran (1215) as the only term which completely and accurately describes the mystery of the Real Presence. Other terms are either incomplete or simply wrong. While consubstantiation affirms a real presence of Jesus, only transubstantiation does justice to the biblical teaching regarding Christ's presence as well as the tradition and practice of the early Church regarding the Eucharist.

This teaching comes from the Bible (Mt 26:26-28, Mk 14:22-24, Lk 22:19-20, Jn 6:32-71, 1 Cor 10:16-17, 1 Cor 11:23-29) and from early Christian writers. Cyril of Jerusalem, in writing his *Catechetical Discourses* around A.D. 350, said that communicants should be "fully convinced that the apparent bread is not bread, even though it is sensible to the taste, but the body of Christ, and that the apparent wine is not wine, even though the taste would have it so." He could not affirm this belief if any bread or wine remained after the consecration.

20 When you get divorced, you are excommunicated automatically and are barred from receiving Communion.

Wrong twice. The Church, as did Christ, does not recognize divorce in the ecclesiastical sense. A valid marriage, once made, can't be undone by a divorce, even if the spouses lose all love for one another. Once married, always married, until death do you part. But the Church recognizes that at times spouses can't and shouldn't live together, perhaps for the good of the children, perhaps for the safety of one of the spouses. In such cases the Church permits the spouses to separate and live apart. It also allows the civil authorities to fix the distribution of marital property and the custody of the children. This is done through a civil divorce.

A civil lawyer, at least one who is not a Catholic, will say the *civil* divorce dissolves the marriage, but that is correct only so far as the civil law is concerned. Marriage is a sacrament and is unaffected by a civil determination. Even Catholics speak loosely of Catholic marriages being dissolved by civil divorce proceedings, but this is sloppy theology. Only death ends a truly sacramental marriage.

Although civil divorce is always undesirable, living together may be even more undesirable. Consider the case of the drunken, abusive husband. The spouses separate, custody and support are fixed by a court—and the marriage continues. Neither spouse is free to marry again.

No ecclesiastical penalty, such as excommunication, applies to divorced people. If they do not attempt to remarry, and if they are otherwise in a state of grace, they may continue to receive Communion. But if one spouse remarries while the other spouse is still living, what the remarrying spouse has really done is to enter into an adulterous relationship. Since adultery is a grave sin, such a person is barred from Communion, since one may not receive Communion while in the state of mortal sin. In our society, in which many Catholics know their faith poorly and find themselves in what they may have thought were valid second marriages, the results can be especially difficult to deal with. But we don't deal with tough situations by abandoning God's sacramental law.

21	**The recent practice in many parishes of receiving Communion under both species (bread and wine) now means that we need to receive under both kinds, or we haven't received both the body and blood of Christ.**

Not so. Whether you receive only under the form of bread or only under the form of wine, you receive both the body and blood of Christ. No matter how small the particle you eat or how small the drop you drink, you receive all of Christ, not just a part of him. You don't receive any "more" of him by receiving under both forms. Receiving under both forms may show more clearly how the Mass mirrors the Last Supper, but there is never any sacramental necessity to receive both.

The traditional practice of the Catholic Church has been to give Communion under one form. The priest alone drinks from the chalice. The rest of us receive hosts only. There are exceptions, of course, but in most parishes that's how it's done.

Fundamentalists think we violate the Bible's injunctions. They cite from the King James Version verses such as these: "Whoso eateth my flesh, *and* drinketh my blood, hath eternal life" (Jn 6:54); "Wherefore whosoever shall eat this bread, *and* drink this cup of the Lord, unworthily, shall be guilty of the body and blood of the Lord" (1 Cor 11:27, emphasis mine). "See," they say, "you Catholics deprive people of half of the Lord's Supper."

The problem stems from Fundamentalists' disbelief in the Real Presence. Catholics believe the bread and wine at Mass become the actual body and blood of Christ. Fundamentalists believe the bread and wine used in their services remain just bread and wine. (Many of them substitute grape juice for wine.) They see the Last Supper as just a supper. We see it as much more than that—it's a reenactment or representation of Calvary. At the same time, the Mass is a sacred meal, based on the paschal feast which celebrated the Jews' covenant with God.

What's more, we don't think that the bread becomes only Christ's body, the wine only his blood. We use the terms body and blood—the one for what was bread, the other for what was wine—because the sacred elements retain their outward appearances. But their underlying reality has changed. Philosophers say that the "substance" has changed while the "accidents" have altered. What is on the altar after the consecration still looks like bread and wine, but no bread is there, no wine is there, because the substance of the bread and wine has been changed. You might say all that is there is Christ, but in disguise.

Since he has been glorified, his body and blood have been glorified. The one can't be separated from the other. One of the chief mysteries of the Eucharist—a mystery being a truth that we can't comprehend fully with our limited human reason—is that each particle of the host, each drop in the chalice, contains the whole Christ. It isn't that his body is under the form of bread, his blood under the form of wine. In fact, the host contains both his body and blood—his entire human nature—plus his divinity. Ditto for the chalice. Granted, this is confusing, and it goes counter to our everyday experiences, but we're dealing here with a miraculous change—and with God. God is not divisible. You can't put part of him here, part of him there. He can be many places at once—on your tongue at Communion time, on your neighbor's, on a million tongues at once—but all of him is on each tongue. This is a conclusion we're forced to by theology, even though it's a conclusion we can't fully understand.

What does this mean practically? It means that someone who receives under one kind only—say the host alone—receives exactly as much of the Lord as the person who receives a larger piece of the one kind. You don't get more of Christ by getting a larger host; you don't get more of him by drinking also from the chalice. You get the whole of him even if you receive only a tiny particle from the hand of the priest. Thus there isn't any need for Catholics to receive under both kinds.

Let's get back to the Bible. John 6:54, as quoted by Fundamentalists, presents no problem because Christ also said, "[W]hoever eats this bread will live forever" (Jn 6:58). There he said it is sufficient to receive under one form only, the form of bread. The same words are used in John 6:51. Again, silence with respect to his blood.

When Jesus spoke to the apostles and said, "Drink from it, all of you" (Mt 26:27), he wasn't speaking to laymen. He was speaking to the first priests, who always, at Mass, must communicate under both kinds. Why? Because for a priest Communion has two purposes. First, it is the sacramental reception of Christ, as it is for us at Communion time. But the priest performs sacrificial duties also, and it is his receiving under both kinds that completes the re-enactment of Calvary. By his actions during Mass the priest must portray the shedding of blood at Calvary. This he does by receiving the blood from the chalice. Fundamentalists don't believe in the Mass as a sacrifice—of course, they don't believe in the Mass at all—so they don't appreciate the double aspect of communicating.

Next we come to 1 Corinthians 11:27: "Wherefore whosoever shall eat this bread, *and* drink this cup of the Lord, unworthily, shall be guilty of the body and blood of the Lord." This is the verse as it appears in the King James Version. It has an important error in it. The phrase "whosoever shall eat this bread, and drink this cup" should read "whosoever shall eat this bread, or drink this cup." All reputable scholars, Catholic and Protestant, agree on this. In fact, the Revised Standard Version, which is a corrected edition of the King James Version, has "or" instead of "and."

In his letter to the Corinthians, Paul insisted a Christian must be rightly disposed to receive Communion. He must not be in a state of mortal sin. Paul said it is sacrilegious to receive Communion under either form if one is spiritually dead. If you eat or drink unworthily, you are "guilty of the body and blood of the Lord." This line bolsters the Catholic view that the whole of Christ is contained under either form. If you unworthily eat the host, you act sacrilegiously toward both the body and blood—which implies both must be present under the form of bread. Likewise for the wine.

22 If two people marry in the Church and never have children, their marriage is invalid.

If that were so, then no couple has a valid marriage until the first child is born, but that makes no sense. We all know that a marriage is fully valid as soon as the vows are exchanged and the marriage is consummated—that is, when the first sexual union takes place. Except when one spouse already has children, every new couple begins with zero children. Some time later, in most cases, a child arrives. But until that child is conceived and born, the husband and wife can't be sure they will have a child, no matter how much they might want one. Perhaps they are unaware of a medical problem which makes it impossible for them to have children.

That said, there is a sense in which the claim is true. If a bride and groom never have children because, right from the first, they never intended to have children, their marriage is invalid—not because of the absence of children, but because they did not meet the requirements for a sacramental marriage. Marriage has two aspects, the unitive and the procreative. A man and woman join themselves in holy matrimony. They perform the marriage themselves—they aren't "married by" the priest. He only serves as the Church's chief witness. Once they give proper consent, the two are married. This consent must include an openness to the goods of marriage—both the unitive ("the two of them become one body" [Gn 2:24]) and the procreative ("be fertile and multiply" [Gn 1:28]). If this openness is absent, the consent is imperfect, and no sacramental marriage results. Although the parties live together, they aren't really husband and wife. They have no marriage.

Another point. Some people think that married people aren't really Catholic unless they have many children. Children, of course, are a great blessing, and it is a wonderful thing to see large families. But not every couple is able to have many—or even any—children. The validity of the marriage and the worth of married people as Catholics are not measured by the number of their offspring. As Pope Paul VI discussed in his 1968 encyclical *On Human Life (Humanae Vitae)*, every marriage must remain open to new life, and that is all that God requires. This openness means that contraception is always a grave evil and is never morally right. Yet, if there are serious circumstances (such as the poor health of the mother), parents may limit the number of children they have through abstinence or natural family planning, which takes account of a woman's natural infertile periods but does not, as contraception does, eliminate all openness to new life.

23

Everyone knows that an annulment is really the Catholic equivalent of a civil divorce. Only the words are different.

If so, then "everyone" is mistaken. Let's get our terms straight. A divorce is said to end a valid marriage, but a declaration of annulment says there was no valid marriage in the first place. Even the civil law recognizes the distinction. In every state the civil law provides for annulment in cases where no valid consent has been given by one party. The classic case is that of the drunken sailor who sobers up to discover himself "married." The law says he really isn't married because marriage requires a knowing consent, and a seriously intoxicated person can't consent to anything, since consent requires a clear mind. Likewise, "shotgun weddings" can be annulled because no free consent is given if the groom "consents" to the wedding only to save his life.

That's the civil law on annulments. Church law is similar. For a valid, sacramental marriage to take place, both parties must be capable of giving consent, and both then must consent. Since a child is incapable of consenting to marriage, any attempted marriage by a child is invalid. And adults, though generally capable of giving consent, may not give authentic consent in particular circumstances.

A sacramental marriage requires, for instance, a lifelong commitment and an openness to children. This is part of the consent to a sacramental, permanent marriage. If one party participates in the wedding ceremony with no intention to have a lasting marriage ("I'll give it five years, and if it doesn't work out, I'll leave") or with a refusal to have children, the marriage is invalid from the start, even if the intention is kept secret and the ceremony goes off—excuse the phrase—without a hitch.

So what's the Catholic position on divorce? It is that divorce—the ending of a truly sacramental marriage—is never possible. Ecclesiastical and civil law parallel one another on annulment, but they are entirely different on divorce, because the Church recognizes that a sacramental marriage can be ended only by the death of one of the spouses. Civil divorces, which adjudicate child custody and the division of marital property, are permitted to Catholics, but they do not end the marriage. In the eyes of the Church, civil divorces are really just legal separations. This means that Catholics who are "divorced" are really still married to one another—they're just living apart—and neither spouse may "marry" someone else until the other spouse dies. Any such attempted marriage is no marriage at all. It is plain old adultery.

24 Conscience tells me what's true or false, right or wrong.

Not really. Conscience is the faculty which warns you you're doing something wrong—or neglecting to do something right that should be undertaken. But it doesn't work in a vacuum. You first have to learn what's right and what's wrong, and that's a job for your intellect. If you learn well, your conscience will guide you well. If you learn poorly, your conscience won't be trustworthy.

For instance, if you learn that stealing is no sin, and if you really believe that, your conscience won't bother you when you knock over the bank. Often someone will say, "My conscience tells me this is right," even though, objectively, the act in question is wrong. The problem is that the person's conscience has been inadequately formed. Although we have a duty to follow conscience, we also have a duty to make sure our conscience has been formed rightly. We do this by following the moral teaching of the Church, through prayer, and through close attention to Scripture. If we neglect these, we will end up either with an empty conscience, which won't be able to guide us rightly at all, or a cramped conscience, which sees sin where there is no sin.

The former condition is licentiousness, the latter is scrupulosity. The one never seems to see any sin except the grossest; and the other seems to see sin, even in innocent things. Someone who is burdened either by no guilt at all or by much guilt should see a solid priest-confessor. These conditions are signs of spiritual malformation, and they can be corrected.

25 We don't need to go to confession because sins are forgiven by praying straight to God.

Christ never engaged in unnecessary acts. He instituted the sacrament of penance or reconciliation, or what we commonly call confession (the terms emphasize different aspects, but refer to the same sacrament). He instituted confession as the ordinary or normative way of having one's sins forgiven. This means that it is the standard way. Yes, sins are forgiven when one sincerely repents and prays earnestly to God. In fact, before you even enter the confessional, you must say a sincere act of contrition, so the very sacrament acknowledges the need for a direct request to God that he forgive your sins. But confession to a priest makes a lot of sense: first, because of our limitations; second, because of the nature of sin.

We all fool ourselves at times. We talk ourselves into and out of doing things. We adroitly avoid unpleasantness, and little is more unpleasant than acknowledging our sinfulness and the particular sins we've committed. When we confess to God privately, we run the risk of only feigning sorrow. We might even fool ourselves into thinking we're really sorry when we're not. No sin can be forgiven unless we're truly sorry for it. Here's where a priest, trained in hearing confessions, can help us see past our pride or our remaining attachment to a particular sin. He can help us ascertain when we're sorry and when we're not. Often he can tell far better than we can. He can give us solid personal advice too.

After all, Jesus knew what he was doing. He gave the apostles and—through apostolic succession—the bishops and the bishops' helpers, the priests, the power to forgive sins: "Receive the holy Spirit. Whose sins you forgive are forgiven them, and whose sins you retain are retained" (Jn 20:22-23). He didn't give them this power—his own power—for no reason at all. He wanted them to use it. Note that priests are able to forgive or not forgive (retain) sins. How do they know which to forgive and which not to forgive? Only by being told the sins by the penitent. Then, after questioning if necessary, the priest can evaluate the penitent's sorrow.

Sometimes people today talk about "victimless crimes." In fact there is no such thing. There is always at least one victim, the criminal, and often there are others, known or unknown. The drug pusher, for instance, may have thousands of victims, but may meet only a handful. The adulterer victimizes all the members of the families undermined by the serious sin of adultery. The pornographer victimizes all the readers of a particular magazine, even if they don't realize they're being victimized, even if they revel in it. Just as there are no victimless crimes, there are no sins which affect only the sinner.

Jesus likened our relationship with him to a vine; he is the vine and we are the branches (Jn 15:5). Every branch is related to every other branch through the vine. What happens to one branch influences every other branch. If one branch becomes ill, neighboring branches become ill. Even branches far away are affected. Spiritual illness comes when we sin. It is impossible to sin and not influence others in society. We may not be aware of the influence, but it is there. Since every sin is social in its effects —it affects every other Christian, even every other person—Christ established a social means for forgiveness. In confession we relate our sins and our sorrow to another human being, who represents both our Lord and the whole community of the faithful.

26 Every Catholic must go to confession at least once a year.

Close, but no cigar. The Church's precept about confession is slightly, but importantly, different: Every Catholic conscious of a mortal sin must go to confession at least once a year. This precept or rule of the Church—a violation of which is a sin of disobedience to legitimate authority—is binding on all Catholics over the age of reason. You must go to confession at least once in a year if you are aware of having committed any mortal sin, that is, a grave or serious sin. If you have not committed such a sin, you are certainly not obliged to go to confession. But unless you already wear a halo, you no doubt have committed lesser venial sins and should go to confession to be absolved of them, so you can receive the grace of the sacrament to help you avoid occasions of sin.

Nowadays some Catholics, although acknowledging mortal sin exists, think they are nearly incapable of committing it. Perhaps they have swallowed the erroneous notion that the only remaining mortal sin is a complete rejection of God—hard for even the most wicked person to accomplish. Or they imagine mortal sin as something so heinous they would be locked up for years for committing it. But the "they" could be "we." Mortal sin is much more prevalent than we suspect, and it may well be prevalent in our own lives.

For a sin to be mortal three requirements must be met. First, it must involve a serious matter. Second, there must be sufficient reflection on its seriousness. And third, there must be full consent in the committing of it. What is a serious matter? Many sins listed in the Ten Commandments or contrary to Scripture or the moral teachings of the Church could qualify: murder, envy, abortion, artificial birth control, thievery, adultery, sodomy, fornication—to list only some of the serious sins popularized by the media.

How much time is needed to achieve sufficient reflection on the proposed act? It depends on the sin, but a few seconds often are plenty. You don't need to ponder all day to realize that robbing a bank is a grave sin. What about full consent? It means just what it says. Someone forced into an act doesn't give full consent to it. A drunken person is incapable of giving full consent. A young child is incapable of giving full consent. Ditto for someone asleep, comatose, senile, or held at gunpoint.

FOUR

The Immaculate ✠ Conception, Apparitions, and the Rosary ✠

The Immaculate Conception, Apparitions, and the Rosary

27 | **The Immaculate Conception means that Mary did not need a Savior.**

You might think so, but Mary didn't: "My spirit rejoices in God my savior" (Lk 1:47). Mary acknowledged quite plainly that she had—because she needed—a Savior. Before we examine how she was saved, let's make sure we understand what the doctrine of the Immaculate Conception means.

Some Catholics think it refers to the conception of Jesus. Not so. It refers to the conception of Mary in her mother's womb. Her mother's name was Anne and her father's was Joachim, according to tradition.

We are conceived bearing the stain of original sin, and we need baptism to wash our souls clean. Mary would have been conceived the same way, but God, by a positive act, chose to intervene and prevent Mary's soul from bearing that stain. We are cleansed after conception through the sacrament of baptism. Mary was cleansed in anticipation of her Son's salvific work by a direct act of God.

Here's an analogy. Let's say you're walking along a jungle path. In the middle of the path, carefully hidden by branches and leaves, is a deep pit. You don't notice the pit and fall into it. A passerby pulls you out. You are saved from the pit. Then a woman walks along another path with another hidden pit. Just as she is about to tumble in, a passerby reaches out and pulls her back. She too is saved from the pit, but in anticipation—before falling in—rather than after the fact. Both of you are saved from the pit (original sin), and both have a Savior (God).

28 Catholics must believe Mary really appeared at Fatima, Lourdes, and other sites of apparitions approved by the Church.

Untrue. Catholics are obligated in faith to accept all *general* or *public* revelation, but they are not guilty of sin if they decline to believe in particular *private* revelations, even if those private revelations really occurred. If you find the evidence for a particular apparition unconvincing, you're free to disbelieve in it. In fact, you *should* disbelieve in it, because you'd do yourself a disservice if you believed in something you think didn't occur.

Marian apparitions and apparitions of other saints are examples of what we call private revelations. They are given to individuals in private. General or public revelation is given to the whole Church, is enshrined in Scripture and sacred Tradition, and ended with the death of the last apostle. General revelation is binding on all

Christians, but private revelations are binding only on their recipients. If you ever receive a private revelation in the form of an apparition and are convinced the revelation is from God or from one of his saints on his behalf, in conscience you are obliged to believe in its authenticity and to act on its message. If someone else claims to see an apparition, you're free to ignore it, even if it's authentic.

Belief in the authenticity of a particular apparition is never necessary for salvation. If someone tells you you can't be saved unless you believe in a particular apparition, you can be sure the person doesn't know what he's talking about.

Why do Catholics believe in this or that apparition? The reasons vary. Some are intrinsically stronger than others. Some people believe because they approve of the message. Others believe because they approve of other people who believe in the apparition, or they believe the testimony of the visionaries who claim to have received the apparition. Some folks are impressed with the spiritual signs or effects attributed to applying the message of the apparition. Still others believe because of miracles associated with the apparition. Often several reasons converge in the mind to form a moral certitude of the authenticity of the apparition and its message.

Let's limit ourselves to the issue of miracles as proof, and let's consider Fatima and Lourdes. At Fatima, on October 13, 1917, seventy thousand people witnessed what has become known as the miracle of the sun. Even the anticlerical Portuguese newspapers reported the zigzagging of the sun and the remarkable drying up of the ground and of the witnesses' rain-soaked clothes. It had been raining hard the previous night and into the morning. A few people who were present at Fatima and saw these occurrences are still alive. Not one has come out, after a long lifetime, to say the whole thing was a hoax. Some commentators, then and now, claim the miracle of the sun was an example of mass hallucination, but hallucination is a solitary phenomenon. In medical literature, there are no records of even two people having the same hallucination at the same time, so how can seventy thousand see the same thing, especially when some of them—such as governmental authorities who were atheists—were predisposed to disbelieve in anything smacking of the miraculous?

Fatima is one of those things that can't be reasoned away. An open-minded person either accepts it, based on the scientific evidence, or maintains an agnostic position. There are no grounds for saying the whole thing is a sham. But some people insist it must be, even if they can't figure out how the sham was effected, because they say miracles can't happen. We find, both among Christians and non-Christians, a dogma against the bare possibility of miracles. We may call people who hold such a dogma "anti-miraculists." Their patron saint, if they have one, is Emile Zola (1840-1902), the French novelist best known for *J'accuse*, his intervention in the Dreyfus Affair, in which Captain Alfred Dreyfus was unjustly imprisoned for a crime he did not commit.

Zola took it as an article of faith that miracles are impossible. He maintained that seeing is not believing, and he had ample opportunity to see. He described the case of Marie Lemarchand, age eighteen, whom he saw when she arrived at Lourdes in 1892. "It was a case of lupus which had preyed upon the unhappy woman's nose and mouth. Ulceration had spread and was hourly spreading and devouring the membrane in its progress. The cartilage of the nose was almost eaten away, the mouth was drawn up all on one side by the swollen condition of the upper lip. The whole was a frightful distorted mass of matter and oozing blood." Lemarchand, suffering from tuberculosis, was also coughing and spitting up blood and had on one leg a gaping wound which had defied all attempts to close it.

A physician named d'Hombres saw her immediately before and after she entered the baths at Lourdes. "Both her cheeks, the lower part of her nose, and her upper lip were covered with a tuberculous ulcer and secreted matter abundantly," he said. "On her return from the baths I at once followed her to the hospital. I recognized her quite well although her face was entirely changed. Instead of the horrible sore I had so lately seen, the surface was red, it is true, but dry and covered with a new skin." Other physicians examined her and acknowledged there was new skin on her face.

Zola was present at Lemarchand's return. He had earlier said, "I only want to see a cut finger dipped in the water and come out healed. Then I will believe in the possibility of miracles." The president of the medical bureau at Lourdes brought forth Lemarchand, looked at Zola, and said, "Behold the case of your dreams, Monsieur Zola."

"No," said Zola, turning away. "I do not want to look at her. She is still too ugly." He was referring to the redness of the new skin on her face, the kind of skin one sees when a cut is healing. Within a few weeks her facial sore healed entirely, the tuberculosis disappeared, and the large wound on her leg closed. Marie Lemarchand is one of only sixty-five people officially recognized by Church authorities at Lourdes as having been healed miraculously. As the young woman left the medical bureau, Zola declared to the president, "Were I to see all the sick at Lourdes cured, I would not believe in a miracle."

This is dogmatism gone mad, a complete refusal to examine evidence. It is the antithesis of the scientific attitude, and it is similar even to the attitude of many Christians today. They differ only slightly from Zola. Zola claimed no miracles could occur—ever. Certain Christians claim no miracles can occur after New Testament times—and certainly not in connection with the Catholic Church. Like Zola, they are unwilling to examine the evidence. And there *is* evidence, lots of it, for miraculous cures at Lourdes, for the miracle of the sun at Fatima, and for numerous other miracles, such as the liquification of the blood of St. Januarius, a bishop martyred under Emperor Diocletian in A.D. 304. Some of the bishop's blood has been preserved in a glass container in Naples, and the coagulated material liquifies several times a year. Scientific tests have been unable to explain the phenomenon, which has continued for at least four hundred years.

In a way, the attitude of these other Christians is less logical than Zola's. Zola was an atheist, and he accepted no miracles. But the whole Christian religion is based on a miracle—the miracle of the empty tomb. Christianity depends on that unnatural occurrence known as the resurrection. Without it, said Paul, our faith is in vain (1 Cor 15:14).

29 | We should get rid of the rosary because it's an obstacle to ecumenism.

An understandable assessment, but incorrect. The rosary can be a real bridge between separated Christians, if properly explained.

To begin with, everyone knows about the rosary's existence. If you were to ask what objects are most emblematic of Catholics, people would probably say, "The crucifix and rosary, of course." We're familiar with the images associated with the rosary: the silently moving lips of the old woman fingering her beads; the oversized rosary hanging from the waist of the wimpled nun; more recently, the merely decorative rosary hanging from the rear-view mirror.

The prayers that make up the rosary are highly scriptural. The first, the Apostles' Creed, simply outlines the faith as accepted by Catholics and most Protestants. The Our Father, also called the Lord's Prayer, is strictly biblical (Mt 6:9-13). The next prayer in the rosary, and the prayer which is really the center of the devotion, is the Hail Mary. In the full rosary of fifteen decades it's recited one hundred and fifty-three times. It is probably just coincidental that this is the number of fish the apostles caught when instructed by Jesus to lower their nets (Jn 21:11). Or is it just a coincidence?

Since the Hail Mary is a prayer to Mary, many Protestants assume it's unbiblical. Quite the contrary, actually. Let's look at it.

The prayer begins, "Hail Mary, full of grace, the Lord is with thee." This is nothing other than the angelic salutation given in Luke 1:28. The next part reads this way:

"Blessed art thou among women, and blessed is the fruit of thy womb." Another direct quotation from the Bible, this time Elizabeth's praise of Mary when Mary went to visit her cousin, who was pregnant with John the Baptist (Lk 1:42). To these two verses tradition has added the proper name of "the fruit of thy womb," namely, "Jesus." That gives us the first part of the Hail Mary, and it's entirely biblical. This part of the prayer was used as a formula of devotion at least as early as the twelfth century. The present form was fixed only as late as 1568.

The next part of the Hail Mary is not taken straight from Scripture. It reads: "Holy Mary, Mother of God, pray for us sinners, now and at the hour of our death. Amen." Let's look at the first words. "Holy Mary" should be unobjectionable to all, one might think, but some Protestants do object to it, saying Mary was a sinner like the rest of us. On the other hand, even they acknowledge she was specially favored by God. If anyone other than Christ himself would deserve to be called holy, surely it would be Mary.

Those Protestants and many other Christians will object, though, to giving Mary the title of the "Mother of God." Suffice it to say that the title doesn't mean Mary is older than God. It means the person who was born of her was a divine person, not merely a human person. Jesus is one person, the divine, but has two natures, the divine and the human. Mary did not conceive and give birth to only the human nature of Jesus, but to the whole God-man, both human and divine.

The stickiest line is the last: "Pray for us sinners now and at the hour of our death." Many Protestants think such a request suggests rejection of 1 Timothy 2:5: "There is one God. There is also one mediator between God and the human race, Christ Jesus." This issue depends for its resolution on understanding that, while Christ is the Mediator, he can exercise his mediation however he wishes. After all, he allows us to intercede for one another. Catholics say Christians can pray for one another both on earth and in heaven. Most Protestants say we can do so only on earth. But if Christians in heaven can pray for those on earth, surely Mary, the pre-eminent Christian, can pray for us now, and we can ask her to pray.

The fourth prayer found in the rosary is the *Gloria* or Glory Be. The name is taken directly from the opening Latin word and means, of course, glory. It is a brief hymn of praise in which all Christians can join. It has been used in the Western Church since the seventh century and traditionally has been recited at the end of each psalm in the Divine Office. The last prayer of the rosary is the "Hail, Holy Queen" or *Salve Regina*, the most commonly recited prayer in praise of Mary, after the Hail Mary itself. It was composed at the end of the eleventh century.

Naturally, those Protestants who object to the Hail Mary will object to the *Salve Regina* and for many of the same reasons. The most objectionable line, for them, is probably the third, in which we call Mary "our life, our sweetness, and our hope," a line arising from our honoring Mary as the mother of the Redeemer—recognizing that without her "yes" to the angel Gabriel, the incarnation never would have happened. But these words should be applied to Jesus, not to his mother, they say. But they read into the flowery language of the Middle Ages more than the language demands.

They raise no objection when the young suitor says to the girl of his dreams, "You're the love of my life," even though, to be quite strict about it, the real love of one's life—if the term is taken excessively literally—should be

God, not some other human being. But Protestants don't object to the language of romance because they know what's meant. For the same reason, they shouldn't object to the characterization of Mary as "our life, our sweetness, and our hope" as an expression of endearment.

Each of the fifteen decades of the rosary is devoted to a mystery regarding the life of Jesus or his mother. Here the word mystery refers to a truth of the faith, not to something incomprehensible, as in the line, "It's a mystery to me!" The fifteen mysteries are divided into three groups of five: the Joyful, the Sorrowful, the Glorious. It's common to mean by "saying the rosary" the recitation not of all fifteen mysteries, but of any set of five. Let's look at the mysteries.

First we must understand what they are. They're meditations. When Catholics recite the twelve prayers that form any one decade of the rosary, they meditate on the mystery associated with that decade. If they merely recite the prayers, whether vocally or silently, they're missing the whole point of the rosary. It isn't just a recitation of prayers, but a recitation borne on meditation of the life of Christ and his mother. Critics, not knowing about the meditation part, say the rosary seems boring, uselessly repetitious, and meaningless. Their criticism carries weight if you reduce the rosary to such a formula. It is the *meditation on the mysteries* that gives the rosary its power and its staying power.

The Joyful Mysteries are these: the Annunciation (Lk 1:26-38), the Visitation (Lk 1:40-55), the Nativity (Lk 2:6-20), the Presentation of Jesus in the Temple (Lk 2:21-39), and the Finding of the Child Jesus in the Temple (Lk 2:41-51).

Then come the Sorrowful Mysteries: the Agony in the

Garden (Mt 26:36-46), the Scourging (Mt 27:26), the Crowning with Thorns (Mt 27:29), the Carrying of the Cross (Lk 23:26-32), and the Crucifixion (Lk 23:33-46).

The final Mysteries are the Glorious: the Resurrection (Lk 24:1-12), the Ascension (Lk 24:50-51), the Descent of the Holy Spirit (Acts 2:1-4), the Assumption of Mary into heaven and her Coronation.

With the exception of the last two, each mystery is explicitly scriptural. There are even scriptural versions of the rosary, in which a verse from the Bible is recited along with each Hail Mary. True, the Assumption and Coronation of Mary are not found in the Bible, but they are not contrary to it.

It's little wonder that many Catholics in our day are taking up the rosary again as a devotion, once they understand its scriptural basis and its value as a meditation on the life of Christ and his mother. Even some Protestants are expressing interest in it, indicating this devotion, if properly understood and then explained, can be a real bridge between Catholics and Protestants.

FIVE

Our Eternal Destiny

Our Eternal Destiny

30 **E**veryone is basically good, and almost everyone will go to heaven.

Is that so? Haven't you been reading the headlines? Many people behave as though they're basically evil, including many who never make the newspapers. Is the abortionist a good fellow? How about the drug pusher? What about the incessant fornicator? What about those who seem to build their lives around a particular sin? Have they given their hearts over to Christ—or to their passions?

True, everything that has been created has been created as good, including every person. But we have free will, which we can use or abuse. We all abuse it at times, and we call such abuse sin. "All have sinned and are deprived of the glory of God," said Paul (Rom 3:23). Some people will continue in sin until the end, at which time they will take the down escalator. Others will repent of their sins and die in the state of grace; they will take the up escalator.

How many will be on each escalator? We simply don't know. Scripture doesn't tell us the proportion outright, but there are unpleasant suggestions: "How narrow the gate and constricted the road that leads to life" (Mt 7:14); "many are invited, but few are chosen" (Mt 22:14). When asked by an onlooker whether only a few will be saved, Jesus replied, "Strive to enter through the narrow gate, for many, I tell you, will attempt to enter but will not be strong enough" (Lk 13:24).

The common idea that most people will go to heaven arises, perhaps, from a lack of a sense of the seriousness of sin and from a concentration on God's mercy to the exclusion of his justice. More than that, the idea is that he will save even those who don't want to be saved. God will be merciful, but only to those asking for his mercy. He won't force his mercy or his salvation on anyone. Salvation is a free gift, which, as with any gift, can be declined. We have no good reason to think that there will be only a few decliners. How can we think such a thing, having lived through the bloodiest, cruelest century in human history?

31 Purgatory is not an essential doctrine, but an optional one, just like limbo.

You've made a double mistake. The first is putting purgatory and limbo at the same doctrinal level. The second is saying purgatory is an optional doctrine. Not so. Purgatory is a defined doctrine of the Catholic faith. As a Catholic you *must* believe in it, and, if you are a student of Scripture and early Church practices, you *should* believe in it.

Limbo has a different status. It arises from theological speculation, not revelation. If you find the speculation convincing, you may believe in limbo. If you find the speculation unconvincing, you have the option of not believing in limbo. Probably it's fair to say that there are fewer theologians today writing in favor of limbo than there were fifty years ago. Yes, there are also fewer writing in favor of purgatory—or about purgatory at all—but that is an indictment of them, not of the doctrine.

Why is there less said about purgatory? Several reasons come to mind: the decline in saying regular prayers for the dead; a reduced sense of sin and of our unworthiness before God; an overemphasis, by some, on God's mercy to the exclusion of his justice; perhaps even embarrassment over a doctrine which, at the Reformation, induced some people to leave the Church.

When most people refer to limbo, they mean the limbo of infants, where unbaptized infants are said to go, as distinguished from the limbo of the Fathers, where the good people who died before Jesus' resurrection were waiting for heaven to be opened to them. Since the limbo of the Fathers is specifically mentioned in Scripture (1 Pt 3:19), a Catholic must believe in it. But what about the limbo of infants? It isn't mentioned in Scripture, and the Church never has formally defined its existence, but many theologians writing since the Middle Ages have argued such a state is logically necessary.

The Council of Trent said, in reference to the passing into a state of justification, "Since the Gospel was promulgated, this passing cannot take place without the water of regeneration [baptism] or the desire for it, as it is written, 'Unless a man be born of water and the Holy Spirit, he cannot enter the kingdom of God' (John 3:5)." What happens, theologians asked, to an infant who dies before water baptism and who, because of age, cannot desire baptism? What happens then to one who dies in the state of original sin? If the infant is ineligible for heaven, and if it would seem contrary to God's mercy to punish it everlastingly in hell, how do we resolve the problem? The answer theologians in the Middle Ages came up with is limbo. Most modern theologians see no need for limbo, suggesting that God provides some way for unbaptized infants to make a decision for or against him immediately after death.

Keep in mind that one can be a good Catholic and believe or not believe in limbo, since the Church has issued no definition about its existence. We are not at liberty to label someone a bad Catholic for thinking differently than we do on this subject.

32 Everyone, except for canonized saints and martyrs, must spend at least some time in purgatory before going to heaven.

Not so, though perhaps most people bound for heaven indeed will spend time there. To understand why we must understand what purgatory is.

The Bible teaches that nothing unclean shall enter heaven (Rv 21:27). This obviously excludes the damned, who are unclean because they have no grace in their souls when they die. They are entirely unfit for heaven. But what about those who die in the state of grace, repenting of their sins? They will go to heaven, but not all will go at once. Many will first be cleansed in purgatory, which is better thought of as a state or condition than as a place.

During our lives we often prefer our own will to God's —"Not your will be done, Lord, but mine"—and this preference arises from a skewed self-love. Since God created us, in our beings we are good. In that sense we should display a true self-love. But we display a skewed self-love when we discard God's law and obey our own aberrant wills—that is, when we sin.

If we die with some of that skewed self-love remaining in our souls, we die not thoroughly cleansed, even if we die having repented of our sins. We aren't entirely fit for heaven, but we aren't fit for hell either since we aren't damned. Instead, we will wait in an anteroom of heaven until we are cleansed or purged of the remaining vestiges of that skewed self-love. We call this anteroom purgatory. When the last person on earth dies, and when the last person in purgatory goes to heaven—everyone who goes to purgatory will go to heaven eventually—purgatory will cease to exist.

True, the word "purgatory" does not appear in Scripture, but neither do the words "Trinity" or "incarnation," yet Scripture squares with both, just as it squares with purgatory. But does Scripture mention purgatory directly, even under some other designation? Maybe. Look at 1 Peter 3:19. After his death on the cross, Jesus "went to preach to the spirits in prison." Who were these people? Not those condemned to hell—no use preaching to them, since nothing could help them. Not those in heaven since heaven was not opened to anyone until after the resurrection. These "spirits in prison" were good people, destined for heaven, who had died before heaven was opened through the redemption of the human race.

This verse alone proves that at one time a third state, other than heaven and hell, existed. If that state was purgatory, then Scripture directly mentions purgatory. If that state was not purgatory, then Scripture at least indicates that a third state, apparently much like purgatory, could exist.

The Catholic position is bolstered by 2 Maccabees 12:46, which says, "It is therefore a holy and wholesome thought to pray for the dead, that they may be loosed from sins" (Douay-Rheims). Again, this can't refer to the dead in hell, since nothing will loose them from the penalty they undergo, and it can't refer to souls in heaven, since they already have everything one could desire (God himself) and are perfectly clean. They have absolutely no remaining tendency toward sin. Unless it refers to purgatory, 2 Maccabees 12:46 makes no sense.

Back to the original issue. Will everyone bound for heaven have to spend time in purgatory? No. Only those dying in the state of grace but with a residual skewed self-love will go to purgatory. Very possibly this will be the large majority of the saved. We just don't know, but we can speculate.

Our speculations should begin by looking into our own hearts and asking if we now love God completely, without the slightest attachment to sin. If we can say yes, and are correct in that assessment, and if we die in that condition, we will go straight to heaven. Most canonized saints, theologians tell us, died in that condition—many lived the major part of their lives in it. But if we must acknowledge that some skewed self-love remains, no matter how little, we must conclude that, were we to die now, we would spend the first part of our new lives in purgatory. There we would wait to be thoroughly cleansed so we might suitably be presented at the gate of heaven.

| **33** | The Church dropped its old belief in indulgences—that you can get time off in purgatory by performing some specified religious |

acts and prayers.

No, it didn't. But you need to brush up on what the Church really teaches about indulgences. True, you don't hear much about indulgences anymore, at least not in Catholic circles. If it could be said that at one time they were overemphasized, it's certainly true that today they are underemphasized. Many Catholics simply don't know what indulgences are. That's why they're at a loss to explain the Church's position on indulgences when challenged by "Bible Christians." A few Christians even believe indulgences are "permits for indulging in sin." They don't make that remark in a smart-alecky way. They aren't trying to be cute with the language. They really think the popes have given the okay for licentious activity—provided the right amount of cash is laid down first.

Here we get back to the Reformation. As every schoolboy knows, the Reformation was all about the "sale of indulgences," right? Wrong. The main issues were quite different. The use of indulgences just happened to be a side issue that allowed the movement to get off the ground.

To learn what indulgences are, there is no better place

to turn than to the *Enchiridion of Indulgences.* "Enchiridion" means "handbook," and the *Enchiridion of Indulgences* is the Church's official handbook on what acts and prayers carry indulgences and what indulgences actually are. An indulgence is defined as "the remission before God of the temporal punishment due for sins already forgiven as far as their guilt is concerned." The first thing to note is that forgiveness of a sin is *separate* from punishment for the sin. Through sacramental confession we obtain forgiveness, but we aren't let off the hook as far as punishment goes.

Indulgences are of two kinds: partial and plenary. A partial indulgence removes part of the temporal punishment due for sins. A plenary indulgence removes all of it. This punishment may come either in this life, in the form of various sufferings, or in the next life, in purgatory. What we don't get rid of here we suffer there.

If you uncover an old holy card or prayer book, you'll notice pious acts or recitations of prayers might carry an indication of time, such as "three hundred days" or "two years." Most other Christians, and even many Catholics, think such phrases refer to how much "time off for good behavior" you'd get in purgatory. If you perform a pious act labeled as "three hundred days' partial indulgence," then you'd spend three hundred fewer days in purgatory.

It's easy to see how misinformed Catholics might scurry around for years, toting up indulgences, keeping a little register in which they add up the days and try to get enough so they can go straight to heaven. That's a waste of time because there are no days or years in purgatory— or in heaven or hell, for that matter. The indication of days or years attached to partial indulgences never meant you'd get that much time off in purgatory. What it meant was that you'd get a partial indulgence commensurate with what the early Christians got for doing penances for a certain length of time. But there never has been any way for us to measure how much "good time" that represents. All the Church could say, and all it ever did say, was that your temporal punishment would be reduced—as God saw fit.

Since some Catholics were confused by the designation of days and years attached to partial indulgences, and since nearly all Protestants got the wrong idea of what those numbers meant, the rules for indulgences were modified in 1967. Now "the grant of a partial indulgence is designated only with the words 'partial indulgence,' without any determination of days or years," according to the *Enchiridion*.

To receive a partial indulgence, you have to recite the prayer or do the act of charity assigned. You have to be in the state of grace at least by the completion of the prescribed work. The rule says "at the completion" because often part of the prescribed work is going to confession, and you might not be in the state of grace before you do that. The other thing required is having a general intention to gain the indulgence. If you perform the required act but don't want to gain the indulgence, obviously you won't gain it.

The requirements for a plenary indulgence are tougher than for a partial. After all, a plenary indulgence removes all the temporal punishment due for sins committed up to that time. (If you sin later, of course, the temporal punishment connected with the new sins isn't covered by the earlier plenary indulgence. But, at least, the punishment for the old sins isn't revived.)

"To acquire a plenary indulgence," says the *Enchiridion*,

"it is necessary to perform the work to which the indulgence is attached and to fulfill the following three conditions: sacramental confession, Eucharistic Communion, and prayer for the intention of the Sovereign Pontiff. It is further required that all attachment to sin, even venial sin, be absent."

The greatest hurdle is the last. Making a good confession is not particularly difficult, and going to Communion and praying for the pope's intention are easier still. It's being free from all attachment to sin that's hard. It's quite possible that even evidently good people, who seek plenary indulgences regularly, never, in their whole lives, obtain one, because they are unwilling to relinquish their favorite little sins.

There is an account of St. Philip Neri, who died in 1595, preaching a jubilee indulgence in a crowded church. A revelation was given to him that only two people in the church were actually getting it, an old charwoman and the saint himself. Not exactly encouraging, huh? But don't worry. If you aren't perfectly disposed and can't get the plenary indulgence, you'll at least come away with a partial.

It should be pointed out that the first three conditions may be fulfilled several days before or after doing the prescribed work, though receiving Communion and praying for the pope are usually done the same day the work is performed. By the way, the standard prayers for the pope are one Our Father and one Creed, though you're at liberty to substitute other prayers.

Augustine noted that sinners are punished not just in the hereafter, but in this life (see 1 Cor 11:31-32). In his *Tract on the Gospel of John* he wrote, "Man is obliged to suffer, even when his sins are forgiven, for the penalty is of longer duration than the guilt, lest the guilt should be accounted small, were the penalty also to end with it. It is for this reason that man is held in this life to the penalty, even when he is no longer held to the guilt unto eternal damnation."

What we have to keep clear in our minds is that punishment for sins is not removed when guilt for them is removed. We can be forgiven, yet still have to suffer. For example, a parent might accept a teenage boy's apology and forgive him, but the teenager could still be "grounded" for the weekend. Nothing unfair in that. Suffering can be undergone after death, in purgatory, or during life. It can take many forms here. One form is the ecclesiastical penalty given to us as a penance. Working backwards, the Church came to realize that, since penances can be reduced if the penitent expresses sufficient sorrow and does some pious act, it must be that punishments after death can be reduced the same way.

Paul understood this. He wrote to the Colossians: "Now I rejoice in my sufferings for your sake, and in my flesh I am filling up what is lacking in the afflictions of Christ on behalf of his body, which is the Church" (Col 1:24). We can help one another now. We can help those who are no longer here. And the saints can help us too. If the Mystical Body implies anything, it must imply that. It must mean the saints can pray for us and we can pray for (and do penances for) the souls in purgatory. If it doesn't imply that, then the solidarity of the Mystical Body must be a sham.

From these considerations, said Pope Paul VI in his apostolic constitution on indulgences, came the belief that the Church "could set individuals free from the penalties due for sin by applying the merits of Christ and of the saints." Over the centuries there arose the use of indulgences. This was a deepening of the doctrine of the Church, not a change.

In the earliest centuries penances were severe. Today a sinner might be given a few prayers to recite or some charitable act to perform. Back then a sinner might be commanded to stand outside the church door for a year, asking those going to Mass to pray for him and acknowledging to them his sins. It was a tough regimen. It was one the confessor could ameliorate by reducing the remainder of the penance if the penitent performed some pious act. The penitent's punishment in this life was lessened through a kind of indulgence. Over the years, the Church came to understand that the merits of Christ and the saints could be applied to lessen the leftover punishment that would come in purgatory, the punishment that wouldn't be endured here.

34 | Hell isn't permanent. Eventually all creatures will be reunited with God.

As the anecdote has it, the seminarian asked his professor why Origen (c. 185-254), perhaps the most prolific Christian writer of antiquity, was never canonized. "Good grief, man!" the professor replied. "Don't you realize he believed in the *apokatastasis?*"

The seminarian had nothing to say—and how many would, not knowing what the *apokatastasis* is? At the risk of oversimplification, we can say it's the notion that in the end all people and all fallen angels will return to their pristine spiritual state, that there is no hell, that unperfected spirits, human or angelic, will undergo a process of purgation and then be admitted to heaven. In brief, instead of hell, Origen envisioned a lengthy, but definitely temporary, purgatory. Eventually all would be in heaven, even Satan. Everybody would be saved.

Needless to say, this is not orthodox Christianity. It doesn't square with the Bible, which teaches an everlasting hell for the devil and lost souls. In the New Testament hell is mentioned about thirty times. Our Lord refers to "eternal fire" (Mt 18:8) and "fiery Gehenna" (Mt 18:9). Those who are damned go to "the eternal fire prepared for the devil and his angels" (Mt 25:41). In hell there is "unquenchable fire" (Mk 9:43). Paul wraps it up by saying that when the Lord returns, he will inflict with "blazing fire those who do not acknowledge God and... those who do not obey the gospel of our Lord Jesus" (2 Thes 1:8-9).

There is nothing in these verses to suggest hell is temporary. So how did Origen make such an error? It's a long story, and one not germane to this discussion. But it has to do with his accepting certain presuppositions from Platonism. What *is* germane, and why Origen has been mentioned at all, is that nowadays many people, including not a few Catholics, prefer to think belief in an eternal hell has been little more than an embarrassing and now discardable interlude in Christian thought.

What bothers them isn't so much what constitutes the fire of hell. Even some Fathers of the Church understood the fire to be a metaphor for spiritual pains such as the pain of loss, while others understood it as actual, physical fire. What bothers them is the duration of hell. How can God consign his creatures to separation from him forever?

Keep in mind it isn't so much a matter of God consigning them there as of their consigning themselves there. The damned choose to go to hell by choosing self over God. No one goes there by mistake or inadvertence. The damned damn themselves. God doesn't damn them. They choose their final destination. They remain there, impenitent, unable to repent because they have grown absolute in their hatred of God. All this is a consequence of the most frightening and glorious of our attributes, free will. God allows us to choose him or to choose ourselves. The stakes are high—eternity. He gives us free rein to decide where we'll go. He gives each of us enough grace to gain heaven. Only those who reject the grace go elsewhere.

35 Priests and deacons shouldn't even mention hell. Doing so is uncharitable.

Judging by the content of homilies today, one might think most priests and deacons agree. But not all. One day a Catholic pastor, upon observing the sermon placard of a neighboring Unitarian church, put up his own Sunday homily title by way of reply. The Unitarian minister's sermon was entitled "There Is No Hell." The priest's homiletic reply was called "The Hell There Is."

Was the priest's homily uncharitable, the minister's loving? Many people would say so. Yet, given the practice of Christ himself, the priest seems to come out on top. Consider the Sermon on the Mount. There are five references to hell or damnation in it, yet the Sermon on the Mount is regarded as the most beautiful exposition of charity ever produced. Elsewhere in the Gospels, Christ is no less frequent in his references to hell. "Do not be afraid of those who kill the body but cannot kill the soul; rather, be afraid of the one who can destroy both body and soul in Gehenna" (Mt 10:28). And remember his comments about whitewashed tombs (Mt 23:27) and broods of vipers (Mt 23:33)?

What are we to conclude from these verses—that we are permitted to abuse verbally those with whom we disagree or that Jesus encourages us to consign our enemies to damnation? Obviously not, if we take seriously his words about loving our enemies and praying for our persecutors (Mt 5:44). Still, these biblical examples tell us something about the nature of charity. It means more than smiling at people or making them feel all warm inside. Sometimes it requires, as in the case of our Lord himself, being tough with people. Who is the more charitable, a mother who scolds a young boy for playing in the street, or one who permits her child to do as he pleases because she doesn't want to impinge upon his freedom of expression? Or what would you think of an uncle who was knowledgeable of the stock market yet said nothing about your investing in a company he knew to be unsound, simply because he didn't want to offend your sense of financial competence?

Back to the priest and the minister. Who was the more charitable of the two? If we are to take Jesus at his word that hell is a reality to be avoided, it would be uncharitable not to mention its existence. By warning his congregation of the real possibility of damnation, the priest, rather than the minister, was the true follower of Christ.

36 The Catholic Church teaches we earn salvation by good works.

The Catholic Church has never taught such a doctrine. In fact, it has constantly condemned the notion that we can *earn* salvation. Only by God's grace, completely unmerited by works, is one saved. The Church teaches that it's God's grace from beginning to end which justifies, sanctifies, and saves us. As Paul explains in Philippians 2:13, "God is the one who, for his good purpose, works in you both to desire and to work."

Notice that Paul's words presuppose that the faithful Christian is not just desiring to be righteous, but is actively *working* toward it. This is the second half of the justification equation, and Protestants either miss or ignore it.

James 2:17 reminds us that "faith of itself, if it does not have works, is dead." In verse 24, James says, "See how a person is justified by works and not by faith alone." And later: "For just as a body without a spirit is dead, so also faith without works is dead" (v. 26).

In other words, the kind of faith which is mere belief in a list of propositions is insufficient for justification. Authentic, saving faith is always manifested in good works. And it is those good works which, when they become habitual, keep us from bad works, sins. We lose our salvation when we fall into serious sin. Good works help keep us out of sin, which is to say they help to keep us in a state of grace, and in that way they contribute to our salvation. But the initial justification still comes from faith, not from works.

Good works by themselves aren't enough. The Council

of Trent taught it is impossible for anyone to be justified before God by works, no matter how fine they might be. Catholics who think they can qualify for heaven by praying a certain number of rosaries or attending a certain number of Masses are mistaken. So are those who think heaven is theirs if they engage in lots of do-goodism. What makes us justified in God's sight is faith. If we have true faith, good works follow naturally and protect that faith.

So, far from teaching a doctrine of "works righteousness"—that would be Pelagianism, which was condemned at the Council of Carthage in A.D. 418—the Catholic Church teaches the true biblical doctrine of justification. It avoids the two erroneous extremes. Works alone aren't enough, and neither is a bare faith in a list of propositions.

37 | Reason plays no role in our salvation. We just have to believe.

Faith is a gift from God. You can't earn it, and you can't reason yourself into it. But if you don't use your reason first, you may never grab onto it. Reason has a vital role in Christianity. It has many vital roles, in fact, but a special one at the beginning of one's religious life.

Through reason we can grasp the reasonableness of Christianity. This allows us to overcome stumbling blocks. Even non-believers can come to see that Christianity "hangs together." Such a realization isn't faith, but it is a necessary prelude to faith. Put another way, one cannot be argued into faith, but one can be argued past obstacles to faith.

If Pelagius were stood on his head, his name would be Calvin. It was Pelagius (355-425) who taught that human nature itself could perform all acts necessary for salvation. You could, said Pelagius, pull yourself up by your bootstraps—all the way to heaven. Not so, said Calvin (1509-1564). Your own acts are entirely worthless. Everything you do is worthless. Reason is unavailing since it can't bring you closer to God. Worse, everything you do is a sin.

The Catholic Church says no to both. But it doesn't just take a middle ground, splitting the difference. It takes a higher ground and establishes a higher truth. It says that a knowledge of God and the moral law is within reach of our natural reason, even if reason can't apprehend important truths which are reserved to revelation— such as the doctrine of the Trinity, which we'd never know about unless it had been revealed. With this knowledge of God, we can undertake a natural preparation of the intellect, getting it ready so it will let the will respond properly when moved by grace toward faith. This is what is known as the motives of credibility. Through reason, we can get rid of the distractions and misinformation that keep us from acting on the grace God offers us. Reason itself doesn't produce faith, since faith is an act of the will which is initiated by and then cooperates with God's grace. But reason can remove obstructions to our view. It's here that apologetics has its value.

Paul says, "Ever since the creation of the world, his invisible attributes of eternal power and divinity have been able to be understood and perceived in what he has made" (Rom 1:20). The ability to will and perform good works is instinctive to humanity: "For when the Gentiles who do not have the law by nature observe the prescriptions of the law, they are a law for themselves even though they do not have the law" (Rom 2:14). The good deeds of unbelievers are rewarded (Ex 1:21, Ez 29:18). Christ recognizes the natural love among unbelievers as something good (Mt 5:47).

Grace is a gift from God. Gift is just what the Greek word, *charis*, means. Grace is necessary for the beginning of faith, for perseverance in the grace already received, and for avoidance of sin. Paul ascribes all his virtue and the good results of his work to the grace of God: "But by the grace of God I am what I am, and his grace to me has not been ineffective. Indeed, I have toiled harder than all of them; not I, however, but the grace of God with me" (1 Cor 15:10).

There are two kinds of grace. Actual grace doesn't abide in the soul or sanctify it. You might think of it as a supernatural push toward the good given by God to the soul—a push that enables the soul to do certain things it couldn't do on its own. Faith is due to actual grace and is the first step on the road to sanctifying grace.

Sanctifying grace, which elevates the soul so it is capable of living in heaven, is a permanent quality by which we share the divine life (Jn 14:6, 15:5), become partakers in the divine nature (2 Pt 1:4), receive adoption as the children of God (Rom 8:15, Gal 4:5, Eph 1:5, 1 Jn 1:3, 1 Pt 1:23), and are made temples of the Holy Spirit (Rom 5:1, 8:11). We lose sanctifying grace through mortal sin, regain it through confession, and increase it through other sacraments, particularly the Eucharist.

38 | A Christian can believe in reincarnation.

No way. Scripture teaches, "It is appointed that human beings die once, and after this [comes] the judgment" (Heb 9:27). This means you only go around once in life. You don't get an endless series of second chances. Once you die, you're judged, and you go either up or down—permanently.

In recent years, despite the biblical opposition, belief in reincarnation has become fashionable in some circles, especially within the New Age movement. It has even infected some Catholics. What's the attraction? Perhaps it is the realization that reincarnation gives people the freedom not to worry about amending their lives. After all, if your eternal destiny will not be determined at the instant you leave this life—if you'll get countless chances to reform—you're free to live as you wish. This can be a welcome thought for people trapped in their favorite sins.

Sometimes folks try to find biblical warrant for reincarnation in Christ's words about John the Baptist. In Matthew 17:12, Christ says, "I tell you that Elijah has already come, and they did not recognize him." Matthew adds, "Then the disciples understood that he was speaking to them of John the Baptist" (17:13). Is Jesus saying that John was the reincarnation of Elijah? No. Here's the simple reason. According to 2 Kings 2:9-18, Elijah was taken up bodily into heaven without seeing death. Thus, he wasn't a candidate for reincarnation because he was still in his "original" incarnation.

In Matthew 17:1-8, Moses and Elijah appear to Christ and three of his disciples at the transfiguration. This occurs after John the Baptist has been executed by Herod Antipas. Why is it then that Moses and Elijah appear to Christ and the three disciples, and not Moses and John the Baptist, who, supposedly, really was Elijah? If Christ doesn't mean John the Baptist is the reincarnation of Elijah, what does he mean? Jesus spoke figuratively in Matthew 17:12. He was comparing the prophetic ministry of John in the New Testament to that of Elijah in the Old. Similarly, Luke 1:17 says John "will go before him [the Lord] in the spirit and power of Elijah."

So there's no biblical basis for reincarnation. A person who is considering reincarnation is faced with a choice of believing other alleged sources of religious truth, that is, non-Christian documents, or believing the biblical witness. To accept the former in this instance is to reject the latter.

SIX

Evangelization, ✝ Missionaries, and ✝ Better Homilies

Evangelization, Missionaries, and Better Homilies

39 Catholics don't outwardly evangelize like other Christians because they think actions speak louder than words.

No doubt many think that, but it is no libel to suggest that such an excuse often masks other reasons, including embarrassment and timidity.

No great Christian evangelist has been known for relying only on actions to the exclusion of words. On the first Pentecost, Peter "raised his voice and proclaimed" to the Jews assembled in Jerusalem (Acts 2:14). He preached and wasn't satisfied to evangelize only through setting a good example. In this he followed his Lord, who sent his apostles out in pairs to preach repentance and to heal (Mk 6:7-13). Paul undertook perilous journeys not so Jews and Gentiles alike could make a cool appraisal of his actions, but so they would hear his urgent pleas to convert.

Think of Patrick preaching in Ireland, Cyril and Methodius telling the Slavs about the Christ, Robert Bellarmine arguing eloquently with Protestant Reformers, John Paul II traveling around the world and insisting on the necessity of the whole Catholic faith. They have not been satisfied with actions alone because actions often are misinterpreted. Yes, a person who acts well may be called a good Christian, but for many people that designation today means little.

Consider a true incident: A few years ago an American delegate to the United Nations, when asked by the press how to solve the crisis in the Middle East, replied, "The solution is really quite simple. All we have to do is to get the Arabs and Israelis to sit down together and talk things over like good Christians." The poor man had no idea what he was saying. Arabs, at least the large majority, and Jews are not Christians. They may meet and talk with one another the way good Christians talk with one another. That would be admirable. But, short of conversion, they never will *be* good Christians, no matter how often they mimic good Christians in their actions.

Just before he ascended into heaven, Jesus instructed the apostles and, derivatively, all Christians to "make disciples of all nations, baptizing them in the name of the Father, and of the Son, and of the holy Spirit, teaching them to observe all that I have commanded you" (Mt 28:19-20). He didn't say, "Go out, set a good example, and be satisfied with that." He told us to preach and teach the faith. Evangelization that isn't outwardly visible isn't evangelization at all.

Many other Christians and pseudo-Christians realize

this. They are not afraid to take their messages to members of other religions or of no religion. Think of the street-corner Fundamentalist preacher and the Evangelical televangelist. In fact, the most successful in terms of new converts are precisely those pseudo-Christian sects, such as the Mormons and Jehovah's Witnesses, which emphasize door-to-door evangelization. Catholics are starting to wake up to this fact. It's about time, since about half of all new converts to Mormonism and the Jehovah's Witnesses, not to mention Fundamentalism, are former Catholics.

Catholics first need to evangelize themselves. Most Catholic adults are virtually uncatechized. They may have a professional's understanding of their job duties, but they have only a grammar schooler's understanding of their faith. This is the chief reason they're easy prey for door-to-door proselytizers. The rapidity with which Catholics swallow the most outlandish things told them by such evangelists is an indictment of the sorry state of adult catechesis.

But we should not become depressed. An encouraging reaction is setting in. Catholics who are fed up with their own ignorance are demanding—and getting—the training in the faith they should have had years ago. Many Catholics—some clergy and religious, but mainly lay people—are engaging in active evangelization. One index of their success is the burgeoning number of converts. Some even are clergy from religions which have had a reputation for attracting Catholics. Catholics are now taking a more realistic and effective approach to evangelization, because they are doing it on the biblical and historical record.

40 All Christians agree on essentials, so we shouldn't worry about secondary points of doctrine.

There aren't any secondary points, if you mean by that term doctrines which are inconsequential and can be discarded. All doctrines of the faith are consequential—that is, they matter, and matter deeply—even if some of them are nearer the key elements of the faith than are others. The doctrine of the incarnation is, admittedly, more of a core doctrine than is the doctrine of indulgences, but you can't pick and choose. You can't throw out indulgences and claim to hold the whole Christian faith. Once you start that, the whole edifice collapses, because everything's connected.

The notion of fundamental and secondary doctrines began in Protestant circles, based on the belief that all Christians agree on essentials and differ only in unimportant matters. The problem was coming up with a list of the essentials. That has proved impossible, although there is a sense in which all truly Christian churches—not pseudo-Christian sects—share a core orthodoxy of belief based on the Bible and the creeds. So, even if we can make a rough hierarchy of major and minor doctrines, we don't want to slip into the error of saying the minor ones don't have to be believed simply because they're minor. In fact, Catholics are required to hold and believe all the declared doctrines of the Church.

41 We shouldn't impose our religion on others through missionaries. Our policy should be live and let live.

Well and good, but that's not what Jesus said, although such tolerance seems to be touted as the supreme good in American society these days. He told his apostles to bring everyone into captivity to the truth: "Go, therefore, and make disciples of all nations, baptizing them in the name of the Father, and of the Son, and of the holy Spirit, teaching them to observe all that I have commanded you" (Mt 28:19-20). This is known as the Great Commission, not the Great Imposition. He commanded his followers to make others into Christians through conversion and baptism.

We all must be evangelists. Through our evangelization, we must present the truth of the Christian faith to those who don't yet accept it or who accept it only partially. In doing so we aren't imposing anything on them. You can't force people to believe. You can force them to act as though they believe, true, but you can't force them to believe. Mere acting doesn't count. It isn't what Christ was after. He was, and is, looking for free acceptance of his saving message.

Catholic missionary activity should be seen as an act of charity. Through it non-Christians and other Christians learn about the truths of salvation. They discover that the Catholic Church was established by Christ as the guardian of the sacraments, which are the usual means for obtaining the grace we need for salvation. "Live and let live" is too low an ideal. It often reduces to "Am I my brother's keeper?" (Gn 4:9). In things spiritual as well as things material, we truly *are* our "brother's keeper." Catholics tempted to think they should tolerate every belief and who shy away from evangelization may profit from this "hagiographical note" written by novelist and essayist Dorothy Sayers (1893-1957). It first appeared in

Punch in 1954. The note is about St. Lukewarm of Laodicea, Martyr:

> St. Lukewarm was a magistrate in the city of Laodicea under Claudius (Emp. A.D. 41-54). He was so broadminded as to offer asylum to every kind of religious cult, however unorthodox or repulsive, saying in answer to all remonstrances: "There is always some truth in everything." This liberality earned for him the surname of "The Tolerator." At length he fell into the hands of a sect of Anthropophagi (for whom he had erected a sacred kitchen and cooking stove at the public expense) and was duly set on to stew with appropriate ceremonies. By miraculous intervention, however, the water continually went off the boil; and when he was finally served up, his flesh was found to be so tough and tasteless that the Chief Anthropophagus spat out the unpalatable morsel, exclaiming: "*Tolerator non tolerandus!*" (A garbled Christian version of this legend is preserved in Revelation 3:16.) St. Lukewarm is the patron saint of railway caterers and is usually depicted holding a cooking pot.

42 Priests should speak only positively from the pulpit and shouldn't concentrate on negative things.

Rarely does someone leave the Catholic Church for Evangelicalism, Fundamentalism, or a pseudo-Christian sect out of base motives. Almost always the impulse comes from a genuine, if somewhat misdirected, love for Christ. Often it follows a true conversion—not a mere emotional paroxysm, but a real appreciation, for the first time, of the essential truth of Christianity. There is usually a genuine sense of the absolute necessity of acting on that truth, coupled with a sincere sorrow for sin.

Why do so many who, as Catholics, begin to develop a real appreciation for Christianity—and this is something every Catholic needs to do and re-do, the faith of a child being insufficient for an adult—end up leaving the Church? Why do they today, finally, realize that Christianity must be taken seriously, but tomorrow sign up at the "Bible" church down the street? Often it's because the Christ they're shown at their parish is a wimp. There's no politer way to say it.

If they are told about the life of Jesus, they hear nothing about the cleansing of the Temple (Mt 21:12, Mk 11:15, Jn 2:15). Wimps don't act that way. They live and let live. They hear nothing about Christ's condemnation of the actions of the Pharisees—no "whitewashed tombs" here (Mt 23:27). Nary a cross word comes from a wimp. They hear something about sins they probably don't find attractive anyway, such as theft, murder, and racism. But they aren't told Jesus is annoyed by the sins they like, such as using artificial birth control, fornicating, and getting drunk. Jesus is presented as an indulgent brother, never as the stern judge of the Last Judgment. He comes across as a good listener, but never as one who would say, "Go, and now sin no more" (Jn 8:11, Douay-Rheims). Can they be blamed for not finding him very attractive? Not only doesn't he come across as a God one can take seriously, he often doesn't even seem to be much of a man.

So, when these Catholics finally realize that sin is real and necessitates repentance, that Jesus is God and needs to be treated as such, they discover their Jesus is unlike the Jesus they've been hearing about in homilies at Sunday Mass. And they jump ship, leaving the Barque of Peter.

Don't be too hard on them. After all, how many of us, listening to those sentimental homilies over the years, ever took our priests aside and suggested it was time the congregation graduated from spiritual pabulum to the solid meat of the Gospels?

And don't be too hard on the priests either. Many homiletic experts told them, if not in so many words, to avoid the "hard sayings," to emphasize the I-have-a-friend-in-Jesus approach, to say nothing at which someone might take offense. Shouldn't the experts know what's needed? they thought. We all could have done more, long ago. We know that, now that we're seeing a quiet exodus from the pews, especially on the part of our young people.

And it *is* quiet. Few people who leave the Catholic Church for another make a fuss about it. They just go, though often they return to the precincts long enough to convince their friends and relatives to go with them. It seems the fuss comes from people who have lost their faith but, for quasi-political reasons, insist on staying in the Church and attempt to run it. They refuse to follow the logic of their principles, while the new "Bible Christians" insist on following theirs and so leave Catholicism.

What to do? We should insist on the complete acceptance of reality. As Frank Sheed put it, we should insist on sanity. A man is insane if he doesn't accept reality as it is. One facet—the main facet—of reality is God as he is. To know him more perfectly is to know reality more perfectly, and God is not a wimp. To the extent we allow ourselves to succumb to the notion that he is, we fail to accept reality. We are less than fully sane.

We can begin by opening the Gospels and seeing, again, what Jesus was really like—*is* really like. We can read one of the lives of Christ, whether Sheed's, Fulton Sheen's, Romano Guardini's, or some other. We can learn that the Jesus of the Gospels, the Jesus we worship, is not the Jesus of a Franco Zeffirelli film. Then we can speak with our priests about all this, telling them that a cautious self-censoring is precisely what is not needed in their homilies now.

Edmund Burke astutely noted that as internal restraint lessens within a society, external restraint—meaning laws and punishments—must increase to compensate. The reverse is true also: the more internal restraint, the fewer laws. You can afford the luxury of few laws when people can police themselves. You can't when they can't. It's much the same in talking about the faith. You can afford to talk sweetness and light when the folks in the pews have a solid grasp of God. But when they see God as a wimp, such an approach only confirms them in their misapprehensions. They need to obtain balanced understandings, which can only come through preaching the whole life of Christ, the whole of the faith. If that's done, Catholics who convert as adults—meaning nominal Catholics who finally realize the implications of Christianity—won't be tempted to leave the Church, because they'll know the real Jesus has been taught to them all along.

43 All we can do is pray for better homilies. We shouldn't say anything to our priests since they're in charge.

Prayer is good and necessary, but God expects us to get off our posteriors. A gentle suggestion to your priest might be just what's needed, but make sure it's a suggestion and not a complaint. Here's a suggestion I make when speaking before clergy at priests' study days. Invariably one of the priests asks, "What is the first thing you think we priests can do to advance the faith?" I gave my usual response: Start basing your homilies on solid apologetics.

Most homilies run about ten minutes. Every homily is supposed to be grounded in the readings of the day. Sometimes this is done smoothly, sometimes less so. Actually, it's fairly easy to find something in at least one of the readings that hits home apologetically. Paul's writings are especially good for this. There's little excuse for not having a clearly visible connection between the topic of the homily and the readings.

That said, let me define what I mean by an apologetics homily: I mean a homily that clearly and vibrantly explains some aspect of the faith. I mean one that is dramatic and long by Catholic standards. Begin with the last quality. Our Protestant friends, at least many of them, are used to sitting still for a sermon that lasts an hour or more. Many of them stay later for Sunday school—yes, there are adult versions—or they return to church on a weeknight for further instruction. The average Catholic spends forty-five minutes a week at church. Many Evangelicals and Fundamentalists, and a smaller proportion of Protestants in the "mainline" denominations, spend four hours or more every week in church.

If Catholics and Protestants are biologically indistinguishable, we Catholics, with a little practice, should be able to remain on our posteriors as long as Protestants. I'm not asking us to go from forty-five minutes weekly to four hours. I'm not asking for miracles. I'm asking only that we spend fifty-five minutes—the difference coming from a homily that is twenty minutes long instead of ten.

Of course, it isn't the length of the homily that matters so much as it is content. A good twenty-minute homily can pass quickly, just as a good book, no matter how long, seems to be finished far too soon. But a bad homily, the kind taken out of the latest issue of some pop culture magazine, seems eternal, even if the clock advances only five minutes.

What the folks in the pews want is substance and drama. The two go together. By drama I don't mean histrionics. If the substance is present, the drama is present within the material itself. There's a natural drama within the very explanation of the faith. Just explaining what we believe and why we believe it attracts people. It builds on their natural curiosity. But it's advisable to advertise upcoming topics.

Here's how it would work. This week at Mass Father announces that in next week's homily he'll discuss, say, the charge that Catholics worship statues. He'll look at Exodus 20:4—let's assume that's one of the readings—and at the complaint that the veneration of images amounts to idolatry. He'll urge everyone to bring a Bible to Mass because he'll be flipping from verse to verse—some verses in the readings for the day, others not. The missalette alone won't suffice.

Fine, you say. A good plan. But does it work? I submit as evidence the case of a priest in a Midwestern diocese. He prefers to be anonymous, so you'll have to trust me that he really exists. He does, and so does the success of his homilies based on this approach to apologetics. When he was transferred to his new parish, he discovered all the Masses were losing attendance, slowly yet consistently. He was assigned the noon Mass, the only one he has been able to celebrate each week. (He rotates through other Masses; because of his irregular scheduling, he can't introduce apologetic homilies at those Masses.)

His first topic was baptism. He began a five-week series of twenty-minute homilies, the reading for the first week being the baptism of Jesus by John the Baptist. Over the course of the series the priest defined baptism and original sin, explained the necessity of baptism, discussed how baptism is administered, and refuted the charge that only baptism by immersion is valid. Then he went on to other topics. Some are handled in one homily, others take several.

He saw astounding results. The noon Mass had been attracting only two hundred people when he arrived at the parish. In only six months there were five hundred people each week—standing room only. Significantly, the other Masses lost no one to his Mass, for the simple reason that the noon Mass is given in Spanish, all the other Masses in English. Nor did the increase come from other parishes. The additional three hundred people were almost entirely dropouts from his own parish, the relatives and friends who had lost interest and simply had ceased going to Mass.

Imagine what would happen if this priest's success were duplicated in every parish, at every Mass. Our churches would be crammed, and no doubt giving would rise faster than Mass attendance. The priests would be happy because they'd know they were hitting home runs. Everyone would be pleased. Not bad for an extra ten minutes weekly, eh?

SEVEN

Catholic Customs, Devotions, and Disciplines

Catholic Customs, Devotions, and Disciplines

 We should eliminate old-fashioned customs, such as holy water, since they put unnecessary barriers between us and other Christians.

Not if we understand these customs and pass that understanding along to other Christians who are friends and acquaintances.

Enter a Catholic church, and the first thing you see— or at least the first thing you reach for—is the holy water basin, which is called a stoup, at the door. Few Protestants would dream of installing a stoup in their churches, because to them holy water is mere superstition. Protestants think of the sacramental that way because they usually don't know what holy water is or what it's for. Many Catholics don't either.

In itself holy water is unexceptional. It's plain water sprinkled with a little salt. The salt symbolizes incorruption and immortality. It is the traditional preservative, after all. The salt is added when the priest blesses the water. The use of holy water isn't superstitious because Catholics don't believe the water itself does anything. There are no magical properties to it. Put a drop under the microscope, and you'll find nothing but salty tap water. Dip an injured finger in it, and the finger remains as before. Drink holy water and nothing happens. The use of holy water would be superstitious only if Catholics thought the water itself did something, but it doesn't. Blessing oneself with holy water is no more superstitious than placing one's palm over the heart during the Pledge of Allegiance.

What spiritual benefit holy water has comes from the devotion of the people who use it. Anything can be used for good ends, because everything God created is good. Paul wrote to Timothy, "Everything created by God is good, and nothing is to be rejected when received with thanksgiving, for it is made holy by the invocation of God in prayer" (1 Tm 4:4-5). When plain water is blessed by a priest, it becomes holy water. It is then considered fit for religious uses. It is, so to speak, set aside from regular, unblessed water.

To the ancients, washing with water could symbolize internal purity because washing was used to obtain external purity. Water was used for cleansing the body, so it made sense to use it as a symbol of cleansing the spirit. Most ancient cultures used water in their religious rites and in blessings of fields, cities, and armies. The Jews were no exception. Water was used to consecrate priests (Ex 29:4, Lv 8:6): "Sprinkle them with the water of remission" (Num 8:7). It was used before sacrifices were offered: "For ablutions you shall make a bronze laver with a bronze base. Place it between the meeting tent and the altar, and put water in it. Aaron and his sons shall use it in washing their hands and feet" (Ex 30:18-19). In Solomon's Temple there were ten giant basins of water (1 Kgs 7:38-39).

The Catholic Church uses water not just at the entrances to churches, of course. Water is used in baptism and symbolizes the cleansing from sin that the sacrament effects. On Holy Thursday Christ's example is followed, and feet are washed (Jn 13:4-10). In the Mass, a little water is mixed with the wine prior to the consecration, in memory of the water and blood that flowed out of Jesus' side when the soldier pierced him (Jn 19:34).

For people who object to it, the real problem with holy water, as with other sacramentals and with the sacraments themselves, is that they don't think material things can be used to transfer grace or should have any real part in worship. To the extent they hold to this, theirs is a spare religion. It has no ceremony, no liturgy in the proper sense, no use for what is taken to be rigmarole. But don't think they have stripped religion to the bare-bones requirements of the Bible, even if that's what they claim. As the verses cited illustrate, the Bible supports using holy water. A rigorous adherence to the Bible would imply its ceremonial use. No, the antipathy to holy water is another example of how a non-biblical impulse has taken hold in reaction to misunderstood Catholic practices and customs.

45 | Missionaries at my door explained women aren't supposed to wear slacks (Dt 22:5) and

> **that women aren't supposed to cut their hair (1 Cor 11:6, 14, 15). Seems reasonable to me.**

Think again. The first verse reads this way: "A woman shall not wear an article proper to a man, nor shall a man put on a woman's dress; for anyone who does such things is an abomination to the Lord, your God." The other verses say this: "For if a woman does not have her head veiled, she may as well have her hair cut off... Does not nature itself teach you that if a man wears his hair long it is a disgrace to him, whereas if a woman has long hair it is her glory, because long hair has been given for a covering?" Note that Deuteronomy 22:5 says nothing about slacks, dresses, suits, shorts, or any other kind of modern attire. It just says women are not to dress as men or men as women. That doesn't mean their clothing may not be similar in style. After all, if we were transported back to ancient times, we might think men and women did dress alike—even pious Jews following the Law. We might think that because there was, in fact, little difference in their clothing.

Henri Daniel-Rops, in *Daily Life in the Time of Jesus*, noted that "the same words, coat, cloak, and belt, are used indifferently for male and for female garments; and yet there must have been a difference, since the Law utterly forbade men to wear women's clothes and women to wear men's, and since it is clear from the Talmud that doing so gave rise to the suspicion of homosexuality." Most probably the distinction would have been in the greater fineness of the stuff used for women's clothes, and their more ample cut. We learn from the tractate *Shabbath*, so valuable for information upon costume, that women also wore ribbons made of wool and silk, shawls tied over their shoulders, plaited strands, and a variety of ornaments whose utility seems no more evident than that of some of the objects worn at present.

Some Catholic Bibles, in their notes, remark that Deuteronomy 22:5 may be an allusion to immoral practices in Canaanite religions. What those practices were will be left to the imagination. Suffice it to say that the whole thrust of the verse is that there is a natural difference between men and women that should be manifested in their clothing, but no particular kind of clothing is mandated.

When people conclude that today's women may not wear slacks, they conclude far too much. They read far more into the passage than it warrants. First, it says nothing about what kinds of clothing are reserved (for all time?) for men, what kinds are reserved for women. No Westerners today wear what the ancient Jews wore, so one could argue that all modern men and women, even those dressed conservatively, violate this biblical injunction. Maybe so, but no matter, since it was a disciplinary rule under the old Law and simply doesn't apply today.

Similarly for hair length. Note the claim is that women aren't supposed to cut their hair at all. Even Paul didn't go that far. He merely wrote against long-haired men and short-haired women, but in that he was writing about a particular custom of his times. Hair length is itself indifferent. Most women in even the strictest Fundamentalist churches acknowledge this in practice, even if they don't in theory, because they do, in fact, cut their hair fairly short, at least by ancient standards.

These two issues demonstrate what happens when purely disciplinary rules are taken to absurd lengths and when rules meant for an earlier time are applied indiscriminately to a later one. This is private interpretation gone haywire, to the entire exclusion of common sense. There is a certain consistency to it, though. If a person concludes the Bible is to be taken at face value in all it says, interpretation becomes easy, so long as one verse is read at a time—and so long as some parts of the Bible are not read at all.

The common-sense application of a passage is usually the right one. Passages that seem not to apply to the modern world usually don't. Don't let your acquaintances convince you otherwise. If you feel stumped, repair to a good Catholic commentary, and check the notes in a Catholic version of the Bible as well. Having a few reference works on hand, such as Daniel-Rops' book, will help too.

46 — Priestly celibacy is unnatural and unnecessary in the modern world. The pope should just let priests marry.

Celibacy—the state of being unmarried—has been the state of countless millions of people. Many of them have been in religious life, but most have not. Many people never marry, whether out of choice or circumstances. Their condition is not unnatural. Properly speaking, there are three vocations in life: religious, married, and single. Each is to be treasured, and each person is called to one of these vocations.

There is a growing number of religious vocations today —a fact that may surprise American Catholics. In most of the world vocations are up substantially, but they continue to lag in North America and Europe. Even there the trends are encouraging, compared to what they were just a decade ago. But worldwide vocations are booming.

If we look at the sorts of people, men and women, who are entering religious life, we find very few who grumble about spending the rest of their lives unmarried. Is something wrong with these folks? Do they have a low opinion of marriage? Not at all. In fact, they almost universally have a higher opinion of it than do married people. Perhaps a little of the "grass-is-greener-on-the-other-side" idea is at work. They know marriage is a great good. They know that the Catholic Church insists matrimony is a sacrament, ranking the institution alongside the Eucharist and baptism.

Yet they freely embrace celibacy because they want to devote their complete energies to God and to the service of his Church. They follow Paul's own example by making this sacrifice. Paul recommended celibacy for those called to that vocation, without depreciating marriage in any way (1 Cor 7:8). As our world tends to give less and less value to marriage—the divorce and "living together" statistics are revealing—a counterthrust is coming from, of all places, the ranks of the unmarried religious, whether priests, sisters, or brothers. This is not at all to discount the important role of the married laity. But we should give special credit to those who value marriage highly and, as a sign to the world, voluntarily forego it in order to serve God more wholeheartedly.

There is another fact about celibacy that surprises even many Catholics: It has not been a rule for all Catholic priests. In the Eastern Rites, married men can be ordained. This has been the custom from early times. Once ordained, though, an unmarried priest may not marry; a married priest, if widowed, may not remarry. Marriage is possible only for priests in the Eastern Rites. All monks in the East are celibate, and Eastern Rite bishops are always chosen from the ranks of the monks, which means all Eastern Rite bishops are unmarried.

In the West, of course, the rule has been different. In the very beginning, some priests and bishops were taken from the ranks of the married. The practices in the West and East were the same at this point. But celibacy was soon preferred, and eventually it became mandatory. By the early Middle Ages, the rule of celibacy, in the Latin or Western Rite, was firmly in place. Note that this was and is a disciplinary rule, not a doctrine. The change in the rule did not imply a change of doctrine. In recent years, we have seen a few married Latin Rite priests. Some have been Lutheran ministers who were married at the time of their conversion to Catholicism. More recently, a few dozen married Episcopal clergymen have been ordained as Catholic priests. These are clearly exceptions to the rule.

Most Protestants do not approve of what they refer to as "mandatory celibacy," with emphasis on the adjective, as though the Church were imposing a discipline against the will of prospective priests. They have a number of arguments against celibacy. They say, first of all, that celibacy is unnatural. After all, they claim, God commanded all to marry when he said, "Be fertile and multiply" (Gn 1:28).

Not so. "Be fertile and multiply" is a general precept for the human race; it does not bind each individual. If it did, every unmarried man and woman of marrying age would be in a state of sin by remaining single. Christ himself would have been in violation of the commandment.

If you exempt him because of his divinity, you still have John the Baptist and most of the apostles sinning by not marrying. Remember that even Paul, "Bible Christianity's" favorite apostle, was single: "Now to the unmarried and to widows, I say: It is a good thing for them to remain as they are, as I do, but if they cannot exercise self-control they should marry, for it is better to marry than to be on fire" (1 Cor 7:8-9).

Critics note, "A man leaves his father and mother and clings to his wife, and the two of them become one body" (Gn 2:24). This means a man is supposed to marry, they say. But Christ praised those who would not only leave parents, but give up the chance for a wife and children: "And everyone who has given up houses or brothers or sisters or father or mother or children or lands for the sake of my name will receive a hundred times more, and will inherit eternal life" (Mt 19:29). And don't forget those "who have made themselves eunuchs for the kingdom of heaven" (Mt 19:12, Douay-Rheims).

That may be, opponents of the Catholic position say, but Paul insisted a bishop must be the husband of one wife (1 Tm 3:2), and this means that at least bishops must marry. Such a notion betrays an elementary confusion. The point of Paul's injunction is not that a man must be married to be a bishop, but that a bishop may not be married more than once. After all, if a bishop had to be married, Paul violated his own rule. A rule forbidding a man to have more than one wife—which means forbidding him to remarry after being widowed—does not order him to have at least one. A man who never marries does not violate the rule.

In the early years of the Church, because of the scarcity of single men who were eligible for ordination, men who were already married were accepted for the priesthood and episcopacy. As the supply of single, eligible men became greater, only single men were accepted for ordination in the West, in accordance with Paul's "wish [that] everyone… be as I am" (1 Cor 7:7). The East kept to the old custom.

Continuing along the same line, some people cite Paul's comment that a bishop "must manage his own household well, keeping his children under control with perfect dignity; for if a man does not know how to manage his own household, how can he take care of the church of God?" (1 Tm 3:4-5). See, they say, a bishop must be married. If that were the proper interpretation, the logic of Paul's statement implies a bishop must also have children, and all his children must respect him without qualification. Would a married man without children thus be ineligible for a bishopric? Apparently so. Would a married man with children, one of whom does not respect him fully, be ineligible? Again, yes. And how is one to measure the respect of the children, to determine whether it is "full"? Who's to say? This passage really means that a married man, to be chosen as a bishop, must rule his own household well.

Ah, but we know that "forbidding to marry" (1 Tm 4:3) is a sign of an apostate church, say critics. The Catholic Church forbids some people, clergy and religious, to marry, so it must not be the Church Christ founded. In fact, the Catholic Church *does not forbid anyone to marry.* Catholics can marry with the Church's full blessing. The phrase "forbidding to marry" refers to people who declare all marriages to be evil. Some early heretics held this, as did the medieval Albigensians (Catharists), whom anti-Catholic writers, knowing little about them, seem to admire because they happened to insist on using their own vernacular translation of the Bible.

Marriage is not evil in the eyes of the Church. Remember, it is the Catholic Church that claims Christ raised marriage to a sacrament. No Catholic is forbidden to marry. It is true that Catholic priests in the West may not be married, but no one is obliged to become a priest. Marriage is not forbidden to them as human beings, but as priests. A Catholic man is free to choose the celibate priesthood, the married life, or even the single life, which also is celibate. Celibacy is forced on no one.

Relics come from a superstitious age and should be done away with.

Many Protestants shy away from the sacramental aspects of Catholicism—and not from the seven sacraments only. Even many Catholics today misunderstand the use of sacramentals. What many dislike is the mixing of spirit and matter, the transfer of something spiritual, grace, by means of physical things. That, after all, is what the sacraments are. Common material things—such as water, wine, bread, oil, and the laying on of hands—result in the transfer of grace. Much the same can be said of sacramentals, such a medals, blessed palms, holy water, and ashes. The proper use of them accrues grace. And then there are the relics of saints—the great bugaboo.

No Catholic has ever claimed relics have "magical powers." The sacramental system is the opposite of magic. In magic, something material is regarded as the cause of something spiritual. A lower cause is expected to produce a higher effect. The sacraments and, derivatively, sacramentals and relics don't compel God to work in a certain way. Their use depends on God, who established their efficacy. Their effects are divine, not natural, in origin. It is God who sanctions the use of relics; it is not a matter of priests "overpowering" God through their own powers, which is what magic amounts to.

The classic argument against relics is phrased in terms of relics of the True Cross. If all the alleged pieces of the True Cross were gathered together, it is said, there would be enough wood to build a schooner.

What about it? The charge is nonsense. In 1870 a Frenchman, Rohault de Fleury, catalogued all the relics of the True Cross, including relics that were said to have existed but were lost. He measured the existing relics and estimated the volume of the missing ones. Then he added up the figures and discovered that the fragments, if glued together, would not have made up more than one-third of a cross. The scandal wasn't that there was too much wood. The scandal was that most of the True Cross, after being found, was lost again.

Are some relics spurious? Are there fakes? Yes. But in most cases relics are either known to be genuine or there is some reason to think they may be genuine, even if complete proof is impossible. Take the famous Shroud of Turin, which scientists have been examining for some years. The more honest scientists admit their experiments cannot establish that the shroud is the actual burial cloth of Christ. They admit that is impossible. But they also say that they might be able to eliminate the possibility of fakery. They apparently have demonstrated that the shroud was a burial cloth that was wrapped around someone who was crucified in the same manner as Christ, at about the same time he was crucified, and in the same area where he was crucified.

Will there always be room for doubt for those who seek it? Sure. And, if that is the case with the Shroud of Turin, it is more the case with other relics that have undergone less scrutiny. The skeptic will always be able to say, "This might not have been so-and-so's," and we'd have to admit that's true. There might have been a mistake, or fakes might have been substituted for the real relics.

We evaluate relics the same way we evaluate the bona fides of anything else. Did George Washington really sleep in a particular bed? We have to do some detective work to find out. We may never know for sure. We may have to rely on probabilities. On the other hand, we might have incontrovertible proof that could be disbelieved only by the crackpot who insists George Washington never existed at all.

It's the same with relics. Some are beyond reasonable doubt. The authenticity of others is so highly probable that it would be rash to doubt. Others are probably authentic. And some, yes, are improbable—though we wouldn't want to toss out even most of those, in case we err and toss out something that really is a relic. Keep in mind what the Church says about relics. It doesn't say there is some magical power in them. There is nothing in the relic itself or in any sacramental, whether a bone of Peter or water from Lourdes, that has any curative ability. The Church just says relics are the occasion of God's miracles. In this the Church follows Scripture.

Wrong, say critics. Even if relics can be shown to be genuine, we shouldn't venerate them because Scripture is silent about relics. Is that so? Let's look at what Scripture says. The bones of Elisha brought a dead man to life: "Elisha died and was buried. At the time, bands of

Moabites used to raid the land each year. Once some people were burying a man, when suddenly they spied such a raiding band. So they cast the dead man into the grave of Elisha, and everyone went off. But when the man came in contact with the bones of Elisha, he came back to life and rose to his feet" (2 Kgs 13:20-21). A woman was cured of a hemorrhage by touching the hem of Christ's cloak (Mt 9:20-22). The sick were healed when Peter's shadow passed over them (Acts 5:15-16). "So extraordinary were the mighty deeds which God accomplished at the hands of Paul that when face cloths or aprons that touched his skin were applied to the sick, their diseases left them and the evil spirits came out of them" (Acts 19:11-12).

If these aren't examples of the use of relics, what are? In the case of Elisha, a Lazarus-like return was effected through the prophet's bones. In the New Testament cases, physical things (the cloak, the shadow, handkerchiefs, and aprons) were used to effect cures. There is a perfect congruity between present-day Catholic practice and ancient practice. Anyone who rejects all Catholic relics today as frauds should also reject these biblical accounts as frauds.

EIGHT

The Spirit World and Superstitions

The Spirit World
and Superstitions

48 **T**his is a scientific age. We know miracles don't happen anymore.

That's one attitude, but there are others, including the Catholic. The attitude of Catholics, Eastern Orthodox, and some Protestants is that, yes, miracles happen today and have happened throughout Christian history. Some parts of Protestantism, including Fundamentalism and much of Evangelicalism, says miracles *do not* happen any longer. Secularism says miracles *cannot* happen.

Some Catholics have been influenced by the last two positions, especially the secularist. They think even miracles recorded in the Bible are suspect, and they are quite sure miracles cannot happen today. After all, they say, miracles are pre-scientific. Yes, but they are also post-scientific. They occurred before the age of modern science, they occur during it, and they will occur after that age has ended.

The attitude of these Catholics and of the secularists they imitate is really unscientific. It is not based on conclusions drawn from a scientific investigation of alleged miracles. Go to Lourdes, if you wish, or to the site of any other allegedly miraculous occurrence, and you will find no skeptics taking down notes and examining people who claim miraculous healings. They *know* miracles can't happen after New Testament times, so why bother to check?

Their argument goes something like this. When Christianity was just starting out, miracles were used to attest to its credentials. "But they went forth and preached everywhere, while the Lord worked with them and confirmed the word through accompanying signs" (Mk 16:20). But miracles are no longer needed, since Christianity was established firmly enough by the time the last apostle died. They are no longer needed to produce faith because faith is supplied by the Bible.

Cited in support are these verses: "Now Jesus did many other signs in the presence of his disciples that are not written in this book. But these are written that you may come to believe that Jesus is the Messiah, the Son of God, and that through this belief you may have life in his name" (Jn 20:30-31). "Thus faith comes from what is heard, and what is heard comes through the word of Christ" (Rom 10:17).

What do these verses really prove? The apostle John recounted some of Christ's miracles so readers would believe in Christ. That doesn't mean there wouldn't be any miracles for later generations. Some people will believe based on what they read. Others might need that extra push provided through miracles. And the verse from Romans? It's quite true that faith comes through Christ's word, but, again, not everyone is equally open to his word. Some need the added incentive of the miraculous.

Another argument against miracles happening today is that the end of the age of miracles was foretold in 1 Corinthians 13:8: "If there are prophecies, they will be brought to nothing; if tongues, they will cease; if knowledge, it will be brought to nothing." First of all, this verse refers to heaven, where we will enjoy the beatific vision, seeing God face to face. Now, here below, "we see indistinctly, as in a mirror" (1 Cor 13:12). In heaven, there won't be need of miracles to bolster faith because we'll *know*. Second, this verse is selected as proof of the no-miracles-now position because it refers to the cessation of the early forms of prophecy and speaking in tongues. The implication is that all such gifts, including miracles, have ended, but that doesn't follow. Even if prophecy and speaking in tongues did die out forever in the first centuries (we aren't discussing here whether they have reappeared in recent years), their dying out would not necessarily say anything about the gift of miracles. If miracles were needed to get Christianity off the ground, why shouldn't they be needed to keep it going?

The fact is that the Bible nowhere says all miracles ended with New Testament times. Granted, it doesn't say miracles would continue until our own day either. As in so many areas, Scripture is silent here. Why shouldn't it be? Whether miracles occur today is a question for scientific inquiry, not for prejudging. The requisite tools are open and sharp minds.

49 I don't believe in angels as shown on old holy cards. That's just ancient superstition.

Bad art often leads to bad theology. It's little wonder that people who think of angels as fat, winged cherubs can't take the idea of angels seriously. Their problem, of course, is that they take art too literally. It's unlikely that baroque artists who covered ceilings with these rotund images really thought that's how angels look. Could any great artist be that dumb? But if you're going to represent angels artistically, you have to show them as *something*. You can't leave a blank space labeled "Pretend an angel is here."

Traditionally angels have appeared as youths in robes, winged or unwinged, or as barely-clad babies. However inadequate the artwork, the fact remains that angels exist. Both the Fourth Lateran and First Vatican Councils taught that God created pure spirits at the beginning of time. The Bible also affirms their existence: "For in him were created all things in heaven and on earth, the visible and the invisible, whether thrones or dominions or principalities or powers" (Col 1:16). These last four terms all refer to angels. "Principalities" in this context doesn't mean monarchies, it means angels of high rank or position. It's unfortunate that enlightened people today discount the existence of angels. Actually, there's nothing enlightened about such an attitude—quite the opposite: It's a species of closed-mindedness.

We know from our childhood catechism—still a good source of straight thinking—that God made three kinds of creatures. Some are pure matter: rocks, water, air, plants, animals. Others are pure spirits: angels, both the good ones in heaven and the bad ones in hell. And some are a combination of matter and spirit: human beings. We know the first and third kinds well, because the first kind everywhere surrounds us, and we are the third kind. But beings of the second kind, angels, are every bit as real as we are or as the world around us is.

Why do we have trouble imagining them? Because the imagination can produce images based only on what we have seen. Spirits—including God, the angels, and our own souls—are invisible, and that's why we can't, properly speaking, *imagine* them. We can't make accurate pictures of them in our minds. But we can *conceive* of them—that is, we can understand them, to greater or lesser extents, in our minds, even if we can't form a mental image of them.

The word "angel" comes from the Greek word for messenger. It is an appropriate title for Gabriel, who brought Mary the invitation to be mother of the Messiah (Lk 1:26-38). Another messenger from heaven appeared to Joseph and told him, "It is through the holy Spirit that this child has been conceived" (Mt 1:20). Still another told Joseph to flee to Egypt (Mt 2:13). On Easter morning an angel rolled back the stone to the tomb and spoke to the women who came to anoint Jesus' body, announcing to them the Lord's resurrection (Mt 28:2-5). An angel released the imprisoned apostles (Acts 5:19), and an angel instructed Philip to take the road toward Gaza, on which he met the Ethiopian eunuch (Acts 8:26). Of course, a messenger can take messages in both directions. God sent the angel Raphael to Tobit and his daughter-in-law Sarah, and he took their prayers to the throne of God (Tob 12:12). In Revelation 8:4 we are told an angel presents to God the prayers of Christians on earth.

Why are even some Catholics reluctant to believe in angels, given the scriptural testimony for them? No doubt it is a legacy of nineteenth-century scientism, the notion that unless you can weigh or measure something, it doesn't exist. This notion was soundly discredited a century ago, but its effects linger in today's secularism, which affects even believers. A good antidote is immersion in the Bible.

50 | We know now the devil is imaginary.

We don't know any such thing. In fact, we know just the opposite. The Catholic Church teaches the devil is real, not a phantasm or a holdover from scary bedtime stories. In 1975 the Sacred Congregation for Divine Worship issued a document called *Christian Faith and Demonology*. It quotes Pope Paul VI: "It is a departure from the picture provided by biblical and Church teaching to refuse to acknowledge the devil's existence; to regard him as... a conceptual and fanciful personification of the unknown causes of our misfortunes."

If someone tells you something different, he does so from his own mind, not from the mind of the Church. Maybe the devil makes him do it! At the Fourth Lateran Council (1215), the bishops defined that "the devil and the other evil spirits were created good in nature, but they became evil by their own actions." At baptism, adult candidates are asked to renounce Satan and all his empty promises. The Church even has an official rite of exorcism—which would be unnecessary if demons didn't exist. If this doesn't convince you, consider what Scripture reports Jesus said and did (Mt 4:1-11, 12:22-30; Mk 1:34; Lk 10:18, 22:31; Jn 8:44).

He certainly believed in demons, and so did his early followers, the Fathers of the Church. They were very clear on the matter. Irenaeus, at the end of the second century, wrote that the devil is "an apostate angel" who tries to "darken the hearts of those who would serve him." Tertullian, writing about the same time, said "the business [of demons] is to corrupt mankind." And Origen, a generation later, noted that "ecclesiastical teaching maintains that these beings do indeed exist." But not to worry, said Athanasius early in the fourth century. Before the redemption evil spirits had wide powers over people, but now, with the coming of Christianity, "their wiles are put to flight."

How are they put to flight? Through the use of the cross, said Athanasius. He was referring, in all likelihood, to the exorcist's use of the cross to help cast out demons, both in cases of possession and obession. In a case of possession, a person's bodily actions are under control of an evil spirit. In a case of obsession, the person is not touched directly; rather, the demon works on physical things surrounding the person—chairs move, books fall off shelves, odd cries are heard.

As frightening as these occurrences may be, they are not as dangerous as the demons' more common work: temptation to apostasy and sin. "Some will turn away from the faith by paying attention to deceitful spirits and demonic instructions" (1 Tm 4:1). The most frightening kind of apostasy is outright devil worship—uncommon, but becoming less so every year with the spread of modern Satanism—but generally apostasy is milder, less dramatic, yet still dangerous. Usually it manifests itself as a slow, almost imperceptible slide into a life of dull sin.

51 The Church affirms extraterrestrials exist.

Actually, it's silent on the question. Whether extraterrestrial beings exist is a matter for science, not theology. Their existence or non-existence is immaterial, so far as our faith is concerned.

Some writers have speculated about what it would be like for our fallen race to discover a world inhabited by beings which had not fallen. (For a good example of this genre, try *Perelandra*, by C.S. Lewis.)

Is it possible for God to have set up multiple worlds, some fallen, some not? Yes. Is there any evidence, even the slightest, that he did? No.

A few scientists, pandering to the tabloids, claim extraterrestrial creatures *must* exist, based on the likelihood of other stars having planets, of some of those planets having atmospheres like earth's, of some of those earth-like planets spontaneously generating amino acids, of some of those amino acids producing sensate (and finally intelligent) life. This is poor science and even worse mathematics. It can be safely ignored.

What can't be ignored quite so easily is the large number of people, including even some Christians, who claim contact with extraterrestrial beings or with the dead—and sometimes with dead extraterrestrials. This is a popular New Age concept. It often manifests itself in what is called channeling, the transmission of messages from the beyond. Channelers seem to fall into two categories:

people who are involved with the demonic, which means they are channeling not extraterrestrials or the dead, but evil spirits, and people who are con artists. You can identify the con artists fairly easily: They draw big crowds and make big money.

52 | Astrology is just a harmless pastime.

It's superstitious—and potentially dangerous—nonsense, made all the more palatable through New Age proselytizing. There isn't the slightest bit of scientific evidence that the stars and planets influence our daily lives. Even if they did—if, say, their gravitational fields induced headaches or something—the time and date of one's birth would be entirely inconsequential, yet astrology is based on calculations based on the time and date of one's birth. The foolishness of this can be demonstrated by observing the lives of two people born at the same time. Their lives are as different as those of people born under different signs.

Newspapers do their readers a disservice when they print horoscopes. You might not believe in the predictions, but millions of credulous readers do. The more they believe in them, the more insulated they are from the truths of Christianity. To a large extent, today's widespread belief in astrology is a consequence of the loss of belief in Christianity. As G.K. Chesterton noted, when people stop believing in God, they don't believe in nothing—they believe in anything. Astrology can lead to other superstitions and eventually to an entire loss of faith. For Scripture's condemnation of astrology, read Isaiah 2:6, 47:13-15; Deuteronomy 18:9-14; Leviticus 19:31; Acts 13:4-12.

There are Catholics and others, though, who claim that the three wise men were astrologers. In saying this they claim the New Testament accepts astrology as legitimate. Not really. The wise men who followed the star to the infant Christ (Mt 2:1-12) were called in Latin *magi* from which we get "magician." The Latin word is derived from the Greek *magoi*. It could have referred to the ancient version of a snake-oil salesman, but Matthew doesn't use it pejoratively. All we can tell from his account is that these men, whose number isn't known but which tradition sets at three, were skilled in what was then called astrology, though to translate *magi* today as "astrologers" is to give a wrong sense.

They were more like proto-astronomers, not casters of horoscopes for the rich or gullible. An ancient belief held that each person was represented by a star which appeared first at his birth. Given that premise, the biblical account deals not with astrology as displayed in today's newspapers, but with a primitive form of astronomy.

Bibliography

 Note to the Reader:
Numbers in boldface refer to misconceptions in
the chapters indicated.

ONE
The Teaching Church and Its Authority

1 and 2.

Flannery, Austin, O.P., ed., *Vatican Council II: The Conciliar and Post Conciliar Documents*, 2nd ed. (Boston: St. Paul Editions, 1987).

Flannery, Austin, O.P., ed., *Vatican Council II: More Post Conciliar Documents* (Boston: St. Paul Editions, 1982).

3 and 4.

Hughes, Philip, *The Church in Crisis: A History of the General Councils 325-1870* (Garden City: Doubleday, 1961).

3, 4, 5, and 6.

Carlen, Claudia, I.H.M., ed., *The Papal Encyclicals*, Vol. 4: 1939-1958 (Ann Arbor: Pierian Press, 1990).

Jurgens, William A., *The Faith of the Early Fathers* (Collegeville: Liturgical Press, 1979).

Quasten, Johannes, *Patrology*, (Westminster, MD: Christian Classics, 1983).

8.

Dawson, Christopher, *The Formation of Christendom* (New York: Sheed & Ward, 1967).

Chaigne, Louis, *Paul Claudel: The Man and the Mystic* (New York: Appleton-Century-Crofts, 1961).

TWO

The Bible— Its Inerrancy and Authenticity

9.

Smalley, Beryl, *The Study of the Bible in the Middle Ages* (Notre Dame: University of Notre Dame, 1964).

Pope, Hugh, O.P., *English Versions of the Bible* (St. Louis: Herder, 1952).

11.

Most, William, *Catholic Apologetics Today* (Rockford: TAN Books and Publishers, 1986).

13.

Burr, William Henry, *Self-Contradictions of the Bible* (Buffalo: Prometheus Press, [1860] 1987).

15.

Carmignac, Jean, *The Birth of the Synoptics* (Chicago: Franciscan Herald Press, 1987).

Robinson, John A.T., *Redating the New Testament* (Philadelphia: Westminster Press, 1976).

Steinmueller, John, *The Sword of the Spirit* (Fort Worth: Stella Maris Books, 1977).

Tresmontant, Claude, *The Hebrew Christ: Language in the Age of the Gospels* (Chicago: Franciscan Herald Press, 1989).

THREE
The Mass and the Sacraments

17.

Burke, Cormac, *Authority and Freedom in the Church* (San Francisco: Ignatius Press, 1988).

Grisez, Germain and Shaw, Russell, *Beyond the New Morality*, 3rd ed. (Notre Dame: University of Notre Dame, 1988).

18.

Keating, Karl, *Catholicism and Fundamentalism* (San Francisco: Ignatius Press, 1988).

19.

Hardon, John A., S.J., *The Catholic Catechism* (New York: Doubleday, 1981).

Halligan, Nicholas, O.P., *The Sacraments and Their Celebration* (Staten Island: Alba House, 1986).

22. and 23.

Elliott, Peter J., *What God Has Joined: The Sacramentality of Marriage* (Staten Island: Alba House, 1990).

FIVE
Our Eternal Destiny

30. and 37.

Lunn, Arnold, *The Revolt against Reason* (New York: Sheed & Ward, 1951).

31.

Sheed, Frank, *Theology for Beginners* (Ann Arbor: Servant Publications, 1981).

32.

Schroeder, H.J., O.P., trans. *Canons and Decrees of the Council of Trent* (St. Louis: Herder, 1941).

33.

Barry, William T. C.SS.R., trans., *Enchiridion of Indulgences* (New York: Catholic Book Publishing, 1969).

38.

Pacwa, Mitch, S.J., *Catholics and the New Age* (Ann Arbor: Servant Publications, 1992).

SIX

Evangelization, Missionaries, and Better Homilies

41.

Sayers, Dorothy L., *The Whimsical Christian* (New York: Macmillan, 1978).

42.

Burke, Edmund, *Reflections on the Revolution in France* (Chicago: Regnery, 1955).

Guardini, Romano, *The Lord* (Chicago: Regnery, 1954).

Sheed, Frank, *Theology and Sanity* (Huntington: Our Sunday Visitor, 1978).

Sheed, Frank, *To Know Christ Jesus* (Ann Arbor: Servant Publications, 1980).

Sheen, Fulton J., *Life of Christ* (Garden City: Doubleday, 1977).

SEVEN

Catholic Customs, Devotions, and Disciplines

45.

Daniel-Rops, Henri, *Daily Life in the Time of Jesus* (Ann Arbor: Servant Publications, 1980).

EIGHT
The Spirit World and Superstitions

48.

Lewis, C.S., *Miracles* (New York: Macmillan, 1947).

Wilson, Ian, *The Shroud of Turin* (New York: Doubleday, 1979).

50.

Nugent, Christopher, *Masks of Satan* (Westminster, MD: Christian Classics, 1989).